EARLY REVIEWS

"A thoughtful, complex, layered look at how we change and what we need to do to create change in our lives. Arlene Harder gently, wisely and sensitively takes the reader along every step of the way, providing just the right questions, tools and approaches to make the journey fulfilling and satisfying."

Belleruth Naparstek, MA, MFT, author of *Invisible Heroes* and creator of the *Health Journeys* audio series

"Arlene has expressed the art of purposeful living with the clear message that it is indeed the questions we ask that guide our life. After all, the future is but a plan and change is guaranteed. Powerful questions combined with magical metaphors and stories will guide the reader to transformational change in living life on purpose and not settling for problems. Questions lead us into being comfortable with 'not knowing' and realizing that when you may feel lost, you are really just exploring."

Patrick Williams, PhD, Master Certified Coach, Founder of the Institute for Life Coach Training and author of *Becoming a Professional Life Coach* and *Total Life Coaching*

"In attempting to make a personal change, many people thrash about willy-nilly, stumbling along a poorly marked path. They could use a strong dose of Arlene Harder's remarkable book which helps a 'change-seeker' move from haphazard to clearer directions for bringing about a desired change. People can find doorways to inner wisdom and learn to sharpen personal questions that point the way. Harder shows that making changes doesn't require magic, just clarity, courage, perspective."

John Fabian, PhD, author of *Creative Thinking and Problem Solving* "

"Arlene Harder has written a wonderful, insightful book on how to move from the 'Land of Wish-and-Want' to the 'Land of Will-Do.' Filled with fascinating stories and helpful exercises, her advice is intelligent, clear, and easily followed—for those who 'will do' it."

Chellie Campbell, author of *The Wealthy Spirit* and *Zero to Zillionaire*

"Arlene Harder offers a method for engaging the reader that is missing in so many personal-growth books. The simple, but not simplistic, questions she poses encourage an interaction between the thoughts of the reader and the information presented. Thus readers become active, rather than passive, participants in developing the self-understanding that is essential to change."

Ivajoy Draper, PhD, MFT, Hypnotherapist

"There have often been times, earlier in my life, when I could have used the blueprint to change that is described in this book, but nothing like this was available. Fortunately, my latest and best decisions have been determined through the careful step-by-step analysis of obstacles and choices I was able to make by asking myself the questions in this very powerful book. Thank you for writing it."

Patricia Kelly, Radiological Technologist

"Every once-in-awhile a personal-growth book provides a refreshingly new approach to transformation. *Ask Yourself Questions and Change Your Life* is just such a book. Reading it is like having a gentle guide encouraging you to be the kind of person you want to be, and showing you how to draw upon the strength you already have within you."

Judith Sherven, PhD, and James Sniechowski, PhD, authors of *The New Intimacy: Discovering the Magic at the Heart of Your Differences*

Ask Yourself

QUESTIONS

– and –

CHANGE

YOUR LIFE

Stop wishing your life were different
and make it happen

Arlene Harder, MFT

PERSONHOOD PRESS

Ask Yourself Questions and Change Your Life:

Published by
Personhood Press
P. O. Box 370
Fawnskin, CA 92333
800-429-1192
info@personhoodpress.com
www.personhoodpress.com

Library of Congress Control Number: 2007941442
ISBN-10: 1-932181-26-1
ISBN-13: 978-1932181265

Cover design by Christopher Tobias
Book design by Chris Burdett-Parr and Luckie Design

Printed in the United States of America

This book is dedicated to everyone
who gave me advice when
I was writing the book.
I have learned a great deal.
I hope you learn much when using it.

PREFACE

If you are interested in self-improvement, you are probably not a stranger to questions. Your days are most likely filled with questions. Unfortunately, many of those questions are not worded and delivered in ways that foster your progress. They are the nagging voice of the critic — said from you to you with anger, contempt or deep regret. These familiar questions include the following: Why did you do that? Why didn't you do that? What were you thinking? How could you be so stupid? Why are you so lazy? Why can't you be successful (or any other word that would fit here) like your friends? What's wrong with you? Why are you so weak? Don't you have any will power?

This is a small sampling of how questions are often used to stop us from going forward with confidence or looking backward with compassion so we can understand and learn from past choices.

This book is filled with questions of all kinds. The spirit of the questions is to promote encouragement, compassion, self-understanding and to provide fuel for positive action in the future. These are the questions that lead to forward movement even when looking at the past. These are questions that reveal buried dreams and uncover tools to make them come true.

I met Arlene fifteen years ago when I was very vulnerable, having just recovered from cancer surgery. My prognosis was good but I was shaken and needed to draw strength from others as well as myself. Arlene was donating her time helping cancer patients use the power of the mind through guided imagery to promote wellness. Her way of using language in a positive hopeful way was just what I needed to jump start the next phase of my own recovery. Her warmth and caring was balm for the soul.

We became colleagues and friends, both as psychotherapists and as writers who explore ways to incorporate positive thinking without negating the value of facing the darkness of life head on. I watched in awe as Arlene evolved and turned her talents toward writing and producing websites for seekers of a better life. I watched her practice what she preached to make her own dreams come true in her career and personal life. I saw her courage in the face of illness and adversity. I watched in wonder as she tackled and learned the deepest complexities of the computer so that she could share her information freely with people who use her websites. I watched her websites grow and change to reach more people and benefit humankind on a larger scale.

Now she has taken the best of her material and put it into this amazing book that uses questions as the path toward change. I first read the book as an interested colleague but found that I quickly became an engaged student of the process. This is not just a book to read for inspiration even though that is a strong attribute of the material. Arlene's commitment is toward active change so that the reader is invited to be constantly involved in a process of self-examination from every angle of life. There is no way you could experience the questions and not be impacted by the process.

Some questions will engage your intellect, some your heart and soul. When a question hits an emotional nerve, you know there is work to do and this book helps you unravel obstacles rooted in the past. If some questions seem unimportant to the point that you want to skip a section, it could mean that you have already done the work but, more likely, you have found an area where you are resisting the process of changing or even understanding your issues around that area. Questions are powerful even when we think they are unimportant to us. It is almost impossible to stay passive when experiencing a penetrating questioning process.

I became aware, as I read the book, of my own passions that I was pursuing in a haphazard style. There was no way I could interact with this book and not begin to focus my goals and dreams. I didn't feel intimidated. I felt I had a gentle guide encouraging me, appreciating my tiniest efforts while enabling me to find the next step to go forward. I felt empathy for my individual process rather than disdain for efforts that in the past I would have dismissed as unworthy of my potential.

You have most likely come to this book because of your interest in leading the best life you can. This book is a friend that can transport you to new interior adventures, leading to concrete behavior that will change your life to bring it more in line with your dreams and values.

Lynne Goldklang, Co-author of *Count It As a Vegetable and Move On* and *Chocolate for a Woman's Soul*
January 2008

TABLE OF CONTENTS

Preface

Introduction i

Chapter One. 1

What Do I Know About the Process of Change?

No matter how old you are, at some time you will be pulled, pushed, or prodded by pain to leave your comfort zone and move along a path from the Land of Wish-and-Want, through a gate that leads to the Land of Will-Do. Learn how to discard beliefs that hold you captive to the past and allow your true self to guide you along the way.

Chapter Two 23

Who Am I Today?

Whether or not you like who you are today, that's where you have to start. So it's important to be totally honest with yourself, explore the stories you tell about your life, discover all the good things about you, and be clear that you are following your dreams and not someone else's.

Chapter Three 41

How Has My Past Influenced My Life Today?

Use the best from your past and discover how your family, experiences, choices, values, and emotional strengths can help you choose and reach your goals today.

Chapter Four 57

How Do I Want My Life to be Different?

Explore your call to action, the goal that can help you get to where you want to go, the advantages and disadvantages of reaching your goal, the motivation for changing your life, and imagine what your life will look like when you reach your goal.

Chapter Five 81

What Beliefs Might Sabotage My Goals?

We all have hidden resistance and unexamined beliefs about such issues as success and failure, winning and losing, money and time, energy and emotional resiliency.

Chapter Six 101

How Committed Am I to Changing My Life?

There is a gate to change that stands between your wanting to achieve success and your willingness to do whatever you need to do to reach that goal.

Chapter Seven 113

What Can Support My Efforts to Achieve My Goal?

The path to success requires small incremental steps, support from family and professionals, expression of the highest qualities of the human spirit, images, symbols, affirmations and incentives to remind you of your goal and give you encouragement.

Chapter Eight. 141

What Can I Do When I Get Stuck?

The path to success on the other side of the gate to change is never straight, but has bends and curves that can catch the unwary and require a re-evaluation of your goal.

Chapter Nine 157

How Can I Share What I Have Learned?

The journey to change brings you almost to the place you started, but with an enriched life and knowledge you can use to help others in the world.

Appendix

Am I a Perfectionist? I

About the Author

INTRODUCTION

Where am I? Who am I?
How did I come to be here?
What is this thing called the world?
How did I come into the world?
Why was I not consulted?
And if I am compelled to take part in it,
Where is the director?
I want to see him.
  —Soren Kierkegaard

This is a different kind of self-help book. Here you won't find an expert telling you what you need to do to change your life. You won't find three, four, five, or more "easy" steps to success. Instead, you'll find lots of questions.

However, by the time you have finished this book, I believe you will have discovered how important the questions are — and that you already have more answers inside of you than you could ever imagine.

There is no doubt that people have achieved success, or some degree of improvement in their circumstances, by using suggestions offered by success "experts." The problem is that strategies that may have worked for others — like the secretary who scaled the corporate ladder to become CEO, the injured runner who won an Olympic gold medal, the renowned scientist who holds fifty patents, or the couple who resolved deep differences and lived happily ever after — may not work for you. There's a good chance that your temperament, motivation, circumstances, relationships, opportunities, education and world view are not the same as these super achievers. You may need *other* strategies if you are to be successful.

You may also have a slight problem with self-sabotage, for we all carry with us an invisible, expandable "backpack" filled with resentments, grudges, unexamined beliefs, fears, and the minutiae of a lifetime. If you can't extricate yourself from the past, it's hard to apply the "secrets of success" that always seem to elude your grasp.

Who are these experts who have the answer to your life? Chellie Campbell, author of *Zero to Zillionaire*, says you can always identify them because *they* claim that only they have the answer to *your* problems. She calls them "sharks" and if you don't have a strong sense of self, you feel inferior in their presence. Sharks feed on "tuna." These are the legions of people who are sure someone else has the answer for how to live their lives. So you'll often see tuna hurrying from seminar to seminar and buying book after book in the belief that the answer to their lives lies somewhere out "there," any place but within themselves. Being in their presence can be exhausting with their pleas for others to tell them what to do, and their cries of blame when they aren't satisfied with the answers.

Then there are the "dolphins." They may also attend workshops, buy CDs, and read self-help books. But their focus is on learning how they can draw upon their own knowledge to meet their needs. Dolphins enjoy playing with other dolphins and helping one another grow. You know when you're in their presence: You feel good about yourself. May this book help you be more like a dolphin and less like a tuna.

Listening to what others have done to achieve success may

be inspirational, of course, but as a recovering perfectionist who's taken a lifetime to manage the impulse to control almost every situation, I know well that reaching goals isn't straightforward. It is only in retrospect that change seems easy and quick. Those who are going through a transformative process, if they are honest, will tell you it isn't simple. Changing a long-troublesome habit, getting a degree, healing strained relationships, or eliminating persistent negative self-talk takes a lot of time, a lot of effort, and often a lot of money.

If change were as simple as many claim it is, we could all accomplish our dreams with ease and live in a world of peace. We'd all be millionaires and have perfect relationships. There wouldn't be a need for therapists, personal coaches, and mentors. We'd merely follow the "simple" path that would assure success.

Questions as Catalysts of Change

If trying to follow the steps to success that *others* have taken hasn't worked for you, I suggest you try another way — understanding *yourself* better. With self-awareness, together with a little inspiration and perhaps a few suggestions from others, you have an excellent chance of choosing and reaching goals that meet your needs.

How can you better understand yourself? Ask yourself questions!

Our brains are programmed to be hooked by questions, like the ones in this book. They are the same questions I've raised with many of my clients who wanted to — change something they didn't like either in themselves, or in the circumstances in which they found themselves. As they considered a question, I could almost see a light bulb go off over their heads and watch their tension fall away as their answers allowed them to see things from a new angle. Whether or not they acted on that insight was another matter, but at least they had an additional piece for the puzzle in their lives.

Unfortunately, there is a good chance that you weren't taught to ask questions of yourself. From nursery school through graduate school you tried to give the "correct" answers on tests. While those answers may have validity, if they are the only things you learn, your life is limited to what someone else decides you should know or think. When you learn to ask questions, you expand the world beyond school and the limited experience of family and friends.

Most of all, questions that change your life are particularly potent when you switch the pronoun from "you" to "I." For example, imagine I tell you, "I like the shape of the leaves of the tallest tree on your block." If you hadn't particularly thought about it before, what I think doesn't affect you one way or the other. On the other hand, suppose I ask, "Have you noticed the shape of the leaves on the tallest tree on your block?" Your brain perks up a bit. It becomes curious. You are being asked something you hadn't thought about before. So when you next leave your house, there's a good chance you'll check to see which is the tallest tree and pay attention to the leaves.

However, you are even *more* likely to notice the leaves if you change the pronouns in the question. Instead of me asking the question, "Do *you* notice...?," turn the question around and ask "Do *I* notice...?" That is why the questions you will encounter in this book are written as though you are asking them of yourself, for *all change comes only from a personal engagement in the process of change.* You don't change because you read about or watch people change *their* lives. You have to find a way to make a shift within yourself for change to occur in *your* life.

How to Use This Book

There are several ways in which questions are presented in this book. Each chapter title is a question, with the contents of the chapter explaining why that question is important if you want to change your life. Within the chapters are sidebars for additional questions that reinforce the basic questions, as well as suggestions for "taking action."

The questions you will encounter cover a broad range of topics, beginning with CHAPTER ONE, in which you explore what you already know about the process through which we all go when making a change in our lives. Then you ask yourself questions about who you are today, because that's where you have to start. Since who we are today is influenced by where we've been, you'll have a chance to delve a little into questions that allow you to discover in your past both strengths and stumbling blocks to change. Next, you will ask yourself several questions to help clarify what it is in your life you'd like to change and why you want that to happen.

Other questions encourage you to explore the barriers that keep you from moving forward, identify your skills and inner resources, and recognize the qualities you will need as you work toward a particular goal. With other questions, you will be able to test your willingness to reach your goal and discover how to find support when you get stuck. Finally, you will discover that by responding to these questions you can not only change yourself, you can make a real contribution to changing the world as well.

It doesn't matter whether or not you write down your answers. Personally, I'm not a journal writer, unless I'm required to do so as an exercise in a workshop. However, if you come to a question that seems particularly apropos, and if you think writing would help, then write as much as you'd like.

In any case, whether you write the answers or only consider them in your heart, don't expect an easy answer for most of them. To go beyond the boundaries within which you ordinarily operate, you will need to move out of your comfort zone, which means you may find resistance in even *considering* the questions.

If you reflect on the questions in this book with genuine curiosity and thoroughness, it will take time. You're unlikely to know all the answers when you first encounter a question, although you may want to skim the chapters to get an idea of what lies ahead. I suggest you notice your reaction to questions that spark your interest — or, equally important, those that appear "unnecessary" or make you uncomfortable. These may be the very ones that can lead to something important for you to understand.

Rainer Maria Rilke expresses this well in *Letters to a Young Poet:*

> *Have patience with everything that remains unsolved in your heart. Try to love the questions themselves, like locked rooms and like books written in a foreign language. Do not now look for the answers. They cannot now be given to you because you could not live them. It is a question of experiencing everything. At present you need to live the question. Perhaps you will gradually, without even noticing it, find yourself experiencing the answer, some distant day.*

Most importantly, remember that behind every question you answer there will be a reason why you answered that question the way you did. In fact, it is "why" and "how" we have reached our conclusions that determine whether one person puts effort into reaching one goal and another person strives just as hard for something quite different. Understanding the "whys" and "hows" of your life can yield important insights.

Just as questions cause your mind to shift a little from automatic pilot, metaphors draw upon different parts of the brain and allow you to see things in a different way than you normally would. So you'll find a number of metaphors that describe the process of change.

I have included several stories to illustrate how answering questions can lead to the eventual achievement of a goal. With the exception of Patricia, a friend, I have used a composite of clients to present several aspects of the journey to change.

In the APPENDIX you will find a questionnaire on perfectionism. I have added this because it was not until I acknowledged that by trying to be perfect (or close to it) I accomplished less than I do now that my standards are not out of reach.

If you are unhappy with your life — or simply suspect things could be a whole lot better — and if you haven't gotten very far when trying to follow the advice of experts, *become an expert on yourself.* I am sure you will discover what a wonderfully capable person you are, and that you have the ability to become even more capable, lovable, and self-confident.

I invite you to begin your journey of achieving your next goal with questions.

Arlene Harder, MFT
January 2008

CHAPTER ONE

What Do I Know About the Process of Change?

Nothing in the natural world remains the same from one moment to the next. Everything is dynamic, continually changing whether we want it to or not, whether we are a willing participant or not. We are part of that world, and our lives can *expand* in response to the changing moods of each season, or we can *contract* by resisting the change we have been invited to make.

Three Paths to Change

Our lives change for three reasons.

The first, which we experience from time to time throughout our lives, comes from being *pulled* by the invisible force of biology and life-cycle stages to be a different person than we were before. A baby learns to crawl, walk, and run because she is hard-wired to move through those stages. In adolescence we couldn't ignore our hormones and the changes they bring if we wanted to. And the inevitable act of falling in love dramatically expands our view of life in ways we could not know without that experience. Courtship, marriage, birth of children, the launching of grown children, and the onset of old age each present us with different opportunities to evolve, grow and develop.

Not infrequently, when we have been inspired by a new vision of who we can grow to be, and what the world can become through our efforts, we are *pulled* to change. For instance, it is hard to read *Paradigm Found* without feeling compelled to make a genuine difference in the world by following our passion, just as the author, Anne Firth Murray, did when she founded The Global Fund for Women.

> **ASK YOURSELF ABOUT CHANGE**
>
> What is the most significant change I have made in my life?
>
> Did the impetus for that change come from a push from someone or the pull of inspiration and developmental change? Or was it the result of emotional and/or physical pain?

Sometimes, though very seldom, we change because we are *pushed* by someone to become a different person than we've been. If that person is our boss, and our job depends on changing some habit or characteristic of our personality, the odds that we'll modify our behavior are fairly good, provided we're not asked to make *too* significant of a shift in how we see ourselves. In some cases, it may be easier to find another job than change long-ingrained patterns of behavior.

Think about it for a minute. How often have you been successful in causing another person to change through nagging, pleading, cajoling, demanding, beseeching, and otherwise shoving that person in the direction of change you wanted him or her to make? Not often, I would guess. I've certainly done my share of nagging, and even though I'm convinced the changes I want others to make would be good for them — and would definitely make *my* life easier — they resist. I've tried the push approach. It seldom works.

What *does* work is the third reason we change, *pain*. Both psychological and physical pain encourage us to work toward relieving our discomfort and can come from many sources. Your factory is outsourced and takes your job with it. Your spouse announces he is leaving for someone else. You've been given a diagnosis of a serious illness. Your business partner's drinking has escalated. In all of these cases, it's no longer possible to continue living as you have been.

Some of us are very good in putting on blinders, of course, and in ignoring a situation that would drive someone else up the wall. Yet we all have a breaking point. That's why the questions in this book are designed to help you no matter whether you are pulled or pushed to change direction, or whether discomfort you have tolerated until now has become too painful to ignore.

. . . . .

The Chemistry of Change

All change takes place in the brain, a soft four-pound organ that is the control center for how you live. It is the most complex machine in the universe with an incredibly linked network of 20 billion neurons connected to an average of 10,000 other neurons. If you could take it apart, you'd see an amazingly intricate network of trillions of synapses, or neuronal connections, that looks not unlike some vast multi-level spider web. It is estimated that the possible number of on/off firing patterns, as chemicals are passed through synapses between one neuron and another, is ten times ten one million times, or ten to the millionth power!

3

We only use a small fraction of those potential connections, of course. In fact, we tend to use the same groups of neurons over and over, routing old thoughts, behaviors, attitudes, emotional reactions, and beliefs back and forth within the same pathways.

This coordinated pattern allows us to make sense of the thousands of experiences we've had over the years. If every single thing that happened, every word we heard, every picture we saw, every body sensation had to be analyzed and processed from scratch in order to understand it, that would take a very long time, even given the speed with which neurons fire. It's much more efficient for the brain to assign meaning to an experience and create a belief or filter through which the next experience can be accepted or rejected as true and valid.

Soon our *beliefs* (the thoughts we experience when certain neurons are "turned on") cause us to *act* (the body's response

ASK YOURSELF ABOUT
YOUR BELIEFS AND OPINIONS

- Do I believe that what I know now is all I need to know to live my life well? Why?

- If I believe there is more for me to learn, am I willing to find a way to learn it?

- Do I often believe I am "right" and want others to *know* that I am "right?" Why?

- If someone believes deeply in something that is much different from my version of "truth," how willing am I to consider the possibility that he or she might know something I could learn?

- Am I willing to question my most cherished opinions?

in word and behavior caused by the firing of other neurons connected to our "belief neurons") in ways that give us *consequences* we have come to expect (and which we then interpret in ways that reinforce our beliefs!).

However, what happens if the "consequences" resulting from our actions are *not* consistent with our beliefs? Unfortunately, most of us, in order to maintain our internal status quo, tend to *interpret* what we experience in ways that correspond most closely to our beliefs. Since we all wear colored glasses (some darker than others), it is not surprising that the world appears tinged with the same hue.

Unfortunately, the cyclical reasoning of "belief-actions-consequences-belief" leaves little room for maneuvering or being open to new beliefs, which results in the creation of a "comfort zone" in which we operate on autopilot. This allows the brain to do what it's always done, sending the same, or similar, thoughts down the same pathways. True, the cycle keeps us on a merry-go-round, but it's the merry-go-round with which we are most familiar. As long as things are sailing along smoothly, we don't see reason to get off.

However, when we're in pain, or when we've been pushed

IMITATE A CAMERA

Become an objective observer of what is, just as a camera sees without making a judgment that what it sees is "good" or "bad." Practiced frequently, this perspective can help you see things in a new light and open you to new beliefs. Further, it can give you an inner peace that is hard to achieve when you are constantly judging and evaluating everything you say and do—and everything others are saying and doing.

or pulled in such a way that we feel we must change our lives, the brain will need to switch off some of the connections it's been using to keep old pathways functioning and build new ones. When we can turn off enough of the old connections tied to old beliefs, we allow new neurons to fire, which allows the brain to switch on its "genetic machinery" (the ability of the body to create proteins for building new neurons), which causes the brain to change internal connections. Through this turn-off-old and build-new process, our brain's biochemical environment builds new interconnected pathways.

The *willingness* to see things in a different way (to try on a new, clearer set of glasses, if you will) "turns-on" neurons that can allow us to interpret our experiences in new ways (i.e., create a new belief about life), which then allows us to act in a way in which we *expect* to get different results and, not surprisingly, discover they *are* different. Over time, we change our lives by changing the chemical functioning in our brains.

Fortunately, one way you can influence the formation of new pathways is to ask yourself questions. As I noted in the introduction, questions require you to shift from a passive mode to an active mode of thinking. If your brain needs to answer a question that lies *outside* its normal reasoning path, it can't continue using synaptic connections along the *old paths*, as it does when we operate on autopilot and the road to new ideas is blocked. By asking yourself the questions in this book, you are giving your brain new experiences. True, the questions themselves may not be earth-shattering, but in attempting to answer them, you are giving your brain permission to switch off autopilot thinking and lay down new neuronal connections that will, step-by-step, lead to the change you want in your life.

This gradual building of new pathways, leading to new beliefs, leading to new behavior, leading to new results is the consequence of what some people call "Kaizen" steps. Kaizen is a Japanese word that comes from two ideographs, the first of which represents change and the second goodness or virtue. The word is based on the observation that, with few exceptions, great inventions and great change don't arise suddenly out of thin air. Rather, they are the consequence of many quite minor steps that, added together, achieve an impressive goal. You can think of these Kaizen steps as small "first-order changes" that incrementally move you toward a significant goal.

. . . . .

First-Order and Second-Order Change

You may not have heard of "first-order change" and its companion, "second-order change," but you've often observed this phenomenon with water.

A pot of room-temperature water placed on the stove will gradually get warmer until it boils. Likewise, a tray of room-temperature water placed in the freezer can gradually get colder in an ice cube tray until it freezes. The change from room-temperature to *almost* boiling and from room-temperature to *almost* freezing are "first-order changes." The water hasn't changed its fundamental qualities. It is still something we call "water," only warmer or colder than it was. The change is incremental. It's not unlike changing your house from muted to bright colors by painting one room and then another, or losing one or two pounds a month until you've reached the weight you want.

In other words, we experience first-order change when we transition in a *linear* progression to a different way of being in the world over a period of time — by doing something more or less than we had done before, by doing it faster or slower, or by accomplishing it with greater accuracy. To become a different person through this kind of change, we need to follow the road of practice and reinforcement with steps that are tangible and measurable. Gradually we change the brain by turning new neurons on and abandoning old ones. In an organization or family, first-order change allows individuals to get used to one change before they are asked to accept another.

Often we make such gradual progress that we aren't aware we're really changing until one day we meet an old friend we've not seen for a long time and he or she says, "Wow. You've really changed. When I last saw you, you wouldn't have had the courage to do that [WHATEVER IT WAS THAT YOU JUST DID]. What made you change?" You aren't likely to respond, "Oh, I've just been making first-order changes." Yet as you think about it, you realize that you *have* gradually gained confidence to do something that would have been totally out of character to your old self.

ASK YOURSELF ABOUT CHANGE

When have I made a significant change in my life by moving steadily, but slowly, toward a goal?

What did I learn from that experience?

Second-order change, on the other hand, is what happens to water in the moment between almost-boiling and boiling and between almost-frozen and frozen. This is not a small change. It is radical, a major paradigm shift, liquid to vapor, liquid to solid.

This kind of *nonlinear* approach to change is sometimes, though not often, observed in organizations (and with an occasional person). It happens when they shift from one way of being in the world to another through a transformation that occurs in less time than a first-order change might take. For this kind of change to occur, however, we need to think and feel very differently in a short period of time so that we can behave differently in a significant way. This requires a major rewiring project in the brain and happens far less than we'd like.

Instant success is the American ideal and if we don't change quickly, we are disappointed in ourselves. It is possible, of course, that you may be suddenly inspired by a speaker or preacher or author, and when something "clicks" you may see things in a totally new light, a complete transformation of thought that translates into a consistent new action and new perspective. However, if you're hoping for a fast and extreme make-over, you might be disappointed, especially if you're waiting for a bolt of inspiration that can take you from who you are, and where you are, and set you down in another place as a totally different person.

In other words, let's imagine you want to no longer be depressed, or you want to no longer feel you have to control everything. As noble as those goals might be, you aren't going to go from depressed to outrageously optimistic in one day, or from being someone who always argues with your partner to someone who can always keep your cool. It just doesn't happen that way.

It happens like this. You begin by choosing a doable goal that is heading in the direction you want your life to move and you do it. A Kaizen step. Then you choose another doable goal and do that. Another Kaizen step. And so it goes.

Then, although you may not notice the specific action you took that caused the *final* transformation, one day you will be pleasantly surprised to discover that your life *is* different, fundamentally and completely different, than it was before you started on the first step toward change. You may still get depressed once-in-awhile, or you may sometimes get upset over something small, but for the most part you've arrived where you were heading, happier and less angry.

From the Land of Wish-and-Want
to the Land of Will-Do

It may be a long time before you take enough Kaizen steps to get to where you want to go. But it can also be a long time from when you first recognize the need for change before you actually take the first step. For example, for years I've wanted to create a visual metaphor that illustrated this observation. Then one day I awoke with a picture in my mind that I've turned into an internet animation called "Getting Through the Gate to Change." This is how it goes.

Imagine that the "comfort zone" I described earlier when talking about the brain is located somewhere in the middle of a place we'll call the "Land of Wish-and-Want." Here you are fairly contented. If there are problems on the horizon, you're largely unaware of them or give them little thought. At the moment, you have no intention of changing your behavior. Why should you? So far you've adjusted your life to accommodate the minor ups and downs of life. Why should now be any different?

Eventually, however, you can't avoid the pressure of "something" that is trying to push you in a new direction, although at first you may not know the source of that "something." Or it may be that you are experiencing emotional or physical pain and realize life is not as cozy as you thought it was, or "should" be. If the force driving you out of your comfort zone is inspiration, you may not hesitate to move toward an ideal of how you can make life better for yourself and for others. If someone is pushing you, you may *temporarily* shift your attitude or behavior, but there's a good chance you'll find a way to return to doing things the way you've always done them. For that you can thank the ease with which the brain uses old pathways and needs encouragement to create new ones.

In the case of physical pain or disability, there is obviously lots of motivation to find a way to make yourself feel better. If you're dealing with emotional pain, however, you will usually begin by *wishing* your distress, whatever the cause, would go away, or that *others* would do something different so you don't have to. For a period of time you remain hopeful that things will magically improve on their own as you attempt to adjust to the current situation.

When things get worse, or at least no better, you become convinced that the situation should change — somehow. But just as wishing and *hoping* don't make things better, thinking they *should* doesn't help either. You begin to suspect that change may actually require some effort on your part. So you tell everyone that you *want* things to change and *intend* to take action soon. Now you're getting serious. You're not quite ready for commitment to a specific action. But you're talking yourself into the courage you will need if you're to explore what you must do for things to actually change.

What is important to note, however, is that it isn't until you reach the point that *you're willing to do whatever it takes to reach your goal* that you begin the first (Kaizen) steps that move you closer to success. It is as though you go through a series of preparatory steps in the "Land of Wish-and-Want" before coming to a gate in a wall that separates these preparatory steps from what I call a "Land of Will-Do." In passing through the "gate to change," you reach a tipping point when change becomes possible. That is when enough neurons have been "turned on" so that your brain can create a sufficiently efficient pathway for the development of a belief that life *can* be different and that new behavior *will* result in new consequences. Only then can genuine and long-term change take place.

. . . . .

The Heroic Journey

One of the best ways to describe such transformation is through the story of a "heroic journey." This is not the making of a hero as we generally think of it in today's world. We consider someone a hero for rescuing occupants from a burning house. The principal of a charter school in Los Angeles that is surrounded by gangs, violence, and poverty says of her students that, "What they walk through to get to school makes them heroes." She honors that effort by creating an environment where they must meet very high standards. There are many illustrations of "heroes" and "heroines" who come forward and act with courage in a moment of need and who go beyond expectations to make the world a better place.

No, what I am speaking of here is the unfolding story of a person who becomes a hero or heroine through a process of personal change that has been described in thousands of legends, myths, and fairy tales over long centuries.

This journey begins simply enough. The potential hero or heroine, like Harry Potter in all his adventures, or Dorothy in *The Wizard of Oz,* or any individual who eventually becomes a hero or heroine, begins as a regular person who moves through ordinary days in an ordinary life. Well, Harry's not exactly a "regular" person, but he lives a fairly ordinary, if unhappy, life.

Things are humming along relatively smoothly, deep in the comfort zone, when something dramatic happens. A tornado. A visitor from another dimension. A wizened old lady with a secret. A rider on a white horse. A challenge from a stranger. A threat to the community. Whatever it is that happens, potential heroes and heroines are put in a position where they *have to make a choice* as to whether or not they will respond to what is called the "call to action," or sometimes as a "call to adventure" or "call to life." I prefer the term "action" because that's what has to happen if your life is going to change, although you may certainly experience the process as an interesting "adventure" at some point along the way.

An excellent explanation of what happens in the first part of a hero's or heroine's story is given by the scholar Joseph Campbell in his well-researched book *The Hero With A Thousand Faces.*

> *This first stage of the mythological journey . . .*
> *signifies that destiny has summoned the hero and*
> *transferred his spiritual center of gravity from*
> *within the pale of his society to a zone unknown.*

To give you an example of this kind of change, later in the book you will meet Roger, a young man who lived in the Middle Ages and became a hero by accepting the call to action. I am sure that if you think of yourself as you follow his story, you will notice that you, yourself, are somewhere along the path of this journey, perhaps already in a "zone unknown."

. . . . .

Leaving Home With a Backpack

Another metaphor may help explain why it is often difficult to take the steps necessary to get to, and through, the gate to change. You see, all of us are born into a home fashioned from our parents', or other caregivers', dreams, traditions, beliefs, education, and experience. The foundation for this home was built by the culture in which our parents grew up and the age in which they lived. Not knowing anything else, we accepted our lives as the way things should be. Even if there was discord in our family, it was home. It was familiar.

13

It is important to note that no matter what kind of atmosphere there was within the homes where we began our lives that, metaphorically speaking, each room had a window. The windows faced one direction. North. South. East. West. And while corner rooms might provide a view in two directions, our parents, like most people, tended to use some rooms more than others and to like the view in only one or two directions. They encouraged us to like that view of life as well. This doesn't mean that what our parents were looking at was wrong, it was just limited.

When we went outside, even though our horizons were expanded, we were encouraged to focus on some parts of the world to the exclusion of others. So we were taken to some places and not others. We attended one church but not another. We went to one school rather than another. We played with one group of children and not another. This selective experience of the outside world felt most natural to us. After all, our parents' beliefs worked for them. Why shouldn't they work for us?

When we were allowed to leave the house by ourselves, our parents tried to make certain that we would continue to accept their ideas on how we should live. They did this by creating a "container" into which they stuffed all their beliefs, injunctions, and instructions. I think of this container of parents' dreams and goals as an invisible, highly stretchable "backpack" we carried with us wherever we went as children — and continue to carry today.

In this backpack we could find our parents' rules for how to treat others, the kind of education we should have, the religion we should follow, the foods that are best for us to eat, the books we should or shouldn't read, the kind of job that would allow us to reach the potential our parents saw in us, the kind of friends we should have, and the kind of person we should marry.

Then as we ventured farther out into the world, we came into contact with relatives, neighbors, friends, preachers, teachers, pundits, experts, celebrities, and even authors of self-help books who added their opinions to our backpack. This is how you should vote. This is what you should wear. These are the beliefs you should hold. These are the charities you should support. Everyone is only too willing to tell us how to change the way we live if we are unhappy, and how to live even if we are happy with our lives. What is important to note is that accepting, without careful examination, someone else's opinion of how we should live adds more weight than is necessary in this bundle we bring with us everywhere.

Not only is our backpack filled with the opinions and exhortations of others, of course, but we add to it our own dreams, accomplishments, whatever self-assurance we've picked up along the way, values we try to live by, skills, accomplishments, and strengths, all influenced by our temperament. Of course, we wouldn't want to leave out our failures, resentments, regrets, guilt, fears, the memory of traumas and the residue of illness. And we make certain to keep a list of every possession we buy, especially those to which we are attached.

With so much accumulated over the years, we've come to believe that the contents of this backpack define us. By claiming that what we believe, what we own, what we say, and what we do is our "identity," we attempt, mostly unconsciously, to guarantee our place in the world, for no two backpacks are the same.

The ego, whose job it is to protect our identity, has bought into the idea that the *contents* of the backpack determine our identity. Thus the ego makes certain that the pronouns of "me," "mine," and "I" are sprinkled liberally throughout our conversations. Consequently, the contents of the backpack are very important to our ego.

But what happens when we no longer can stay in our comfort zone, when we find ourselves on a path to change, when we aren't sure what to do next and we can not longer find the answers in our backpacks? What happens when the weight we are carrying becomes too heavy? Perhaps then it is time to sort through the backpack and explore whether the admonitions and beliefs we've been carrying all these years still apply to our lives.

Is there a way we can discard unusable items in this heavy piece of the past and replace them with something that more accurately reflects who we *really* want to be? Yes. Do we need to find an "expert" who will tell us the items to keep and those we should discard? No. *We* are the experts. It is up to us to decide what to do with all the junk in our backpacks.

. . . . .

A Room With a View

Let's use another metaphor to describe how you can create new pathways in your brain, keep the best from your past, move out of your comfort zone, take a few Kaizen steps, and move toward a new future.

Imagine that in the house or apartment where you live today you discover a door you've not seen before. On the door is a sign that says, "SILENCE WHEN ENTERING THIS PLACE OF CREATIVITY AND CHANGE." You're not sure what you'll find when you open the door, but you decide to investigate. So you turn the knob and see a staircase leading up to a small, very quiet room with clear windows facing in every direction.

In the center is a swivel chair where you can sit most comfortably and look out toward the world as it is today, and how you imagine the world might be in the future. Best of all, there is a table where you can open your backpack and some shelves where you can sort the load you've been carrying for such a long time.

As you place your backpack on the table, you look out the windows, taking care to look in every direction. That is when you notice two things you never noticed before. First, you realize that everyone and everything is connected with everyone and everything else, including you. Then, you notice that every person has a backpack. Before now, when you have met these people on the street, their backpacks were invisible, just as yours was. You knew you had a backpack because you could feel the weight, but you thought you were the only one burdened by the past. Now, you see that everyone carries a load. Some people are so weighed down they can barely move, and even drag a heavy trunk behind them. Others seem to have had the courage to clean out their backpacks as they got older. They now manage to carry only a small knapsack or

---

TAKE ACTION
Bring A Metaphor To Life

A "room with a view" is a mental space you create in your imagination. To translate that idea into reality, it greatly helps to have a physical space where you can reflect on your life, tap into your imagination, bring up experiences of the past, and project into the future in your mind's eye.

To make this a place where you can comfortably ask yourself questions, bring into this space items that add beauty, serenity, joy and peace. Be sure to include something in your favorite color and some paper for drawing when you are inspired or for writing down your thoughts so you can more easily remember what your true self would have you know.

---

fanny pack, and move with grace and ease as they go about their day.

The idea that you might reduce the weight you've been carrying excites you as you unzip the pockets in the backpack and lay out the contents one by one. This should be easy, you tell yourself. *I finally have a place where I can let go of what I don't want and keep what I do.*

Unfortunately, your ego has come into the room with you. It keeps whispering in your ear, despite the sign requesting silence. It wants to remind you that your identity is contained in your backpack. Thus, if your ego has watched you place great importance on material wealth, it will make certain you don't discard anything that would decrease your possessions. If your ego has watched you achieve social prominence, it will make certain you remember the importance of your position in the community. If you place great value on your opinions, your ego will make it difficult for you to throw out anything that might conflict with your long-held views. If you are convinced that your job determines your importance in the world, your ego will do everything it can to help you hold onto the position. Sorting through the backpack will not be easy with the ego around.

That is why, to make the most of the opportunity this room provides, to learn how you can connect more easily with the people you see from this special place, and to step into the future with fewer encumbrances, you'll have to nudge the ego aside. To do that you will need to express your "true self." This is your essence, the most elementary and distinctive part of who you are. It has been called by many names: the "life force within," the "wise self," your "true identity," your "intuition," your "soul." I will refer to it in this book simply as the "true self." Whatever you call it, it is from within this calm place that change and pure creativity takes place. From this center you experience what it is like to go beyond "doing" and "having" into simply "being."

It's to be expected, of course, that when you listen to your true self, your ego will initially be thrown off-balance. It won't know what to do with instructions for living in which you are not identified by your possessions, power, opinions, etc. You will need to make choices from your true self many times before the ego will relinquish the control it has wielded for years.

When it does let go, as it must if you frequently return to this room with a view, you will discover that it is within your true self that your "will" resides. You will need this inner resolve to sustain the energy it takes to reach a goal. Later, in CHAPTER SIX, you are asked to call upon this "will" to discover whether you are ready to step through the gate to change and do whatever it takes to reach your goal of making a significant change in your life.

Further, as you continue to visit this room of change and creativity, as you pay attention to the quiet voice within, you will learn how to embrace qualities of the human spirit that are needed to reach your goals — patience, joy, gratitude, serenity, tenderness, tolerance, forgiveness, courage, to name only a few. In CHAPTER SEVEN, you will have a chance to learn how you can use these qualities every day to move more easily and confidently toward your goal.

· · · · · ·

You Know More Than You Think You Do

When you stand on the path that lies between now and the future, when you imagine your problems will be solved, you may have only a vague idea of how to move down the path, through the gate, and into the future. You aren't even sure how to begin.

Fortunately, however, you're not as clueless as you think you are, for you've already made hundreds of choices that have changed your life. Some choices have turned out well. Others haven't. Yet from each choice you have learned something.

And as you come to the end of this first chapter, I hope you can see how the process of change — as gradual and unconscious as it may have seemed — has applied to your life in the past, and to the possibility of a new life in the future.

As you continue to read, and to consider the questions in this book, I am convinced that the answers you give can help you be more fully in touch with your true self. Carefully considered, they will help you know the direction in which you want your life to change. Then you will be able to set, and reach, goals that are most consistent with the essence of who you are, with what you want to get out of life, and what you want to give.

BEWARE THE CRITICAL SELF

If you are trying to get in touch with your true self to solve a problem and the answer you seem to hear comes in the form of a strong and critical "should," be careful. If it feels as though your "inner advisor" is a parent who is scolding you for not knowing how to do something it thinks you "ought" to have known how to do (even though you haven't been taught how to do it), that's not your true self.

The answers a genuine inner advisor gives are loving and kind, gently leading you to a solution that is best for you and others.

If you want to change your life, reflect on this question from CHAPTER ONE:

- *What do I know about the process of change?*

CHAPTER TWO

Who Am I Today?

L et's assume you want to change your life in some fairly significant way. You want to lose weight, transform a reserved personality into one you think others will admire, earn a graduate degree, or start proceedings for a long-delayed divorce. Before those things can happen, however, you have to start with who you are today — heavier than you'd like to be, shy, without a degree, still married.

Pretending otherwise is a bit like asking Map Quest to give you driving directions to your destination from a different street than the one you live on, or even from a different city. You may want to be someplace else. You may be heading there. You may firmly believe your life will be better when you get there — and one day you may arrive to find it perfectly to your liking. But today you are who you are and where you are. Even if you're lost, acknowledging that fact can stop you from going around in circles.

The problem with acknowledging where you are, however, is that *you often don't know where you are* because you can't see the wider picture.

Several years ago, when in the midst of a disagreement

with a friend about what I thought was true, and she did not, she said, "You may think your opinion is based on reality, but it's just your opinion. Don't you know that your perception creates your reality?" "No," I responded, "Reality is what is. I am only responding to what is there. You are the one who doesn't see things as they are."

Today I realize she was right. I was focusing on the word "reality" and missed the concept of "*your* reality." I didn't know that what I relied on for the "truth" about the world, was only that which I had seen with my eyes, heard with my ears, and felt in my body. The fact is that all of us accept as "real" and "valid" only those concepts to which we've been introduced and that seem to make sense to us. Therefore, while reality may be what is, whether or not we perceive it accurately, we incorporate into our lives only that part of the sum total of reality that we hold in our consciousness.

ASK YOURSELF ABOUT LIVING FULLY

Do I live my life doing what I like doing so much that it recharges my batteries, even when I'm too tired to do anything else?

If I don't live this way, how have I allowed myself to live less intensely and less fully than I could?

How can I awaken my heart and live with passion?

However, once we recognize that perhaps, just perhaps, everything in our powerful, invisible "back-pack" does *not* accurately represent all of what is, or what is possible, we open the door to moving closer to our true selves and our best potential. And one of the simplest and easiest ways to experience more of what is true (that is, easier once we've practiced this a few times) is to follow the advice we hear all the time. Live in the moment. Be here now. Forget the past. Don't worry about the future. Live with awareness.

All these injunctions are important if we are to move our brains off autopilot. To create new neuronal pathways, you need to stop using the old ones. The neurons of guilt that continue to fire when you cling to memories of the past, and the neurons of worry that are fired when you fear what might happen in the future, can't fire when you stay in the moment.

When you're focused on what is happening now, this moment, you are erecting a detour sign in the brain's well-worn pathways to the past and future. If, rather than going down those roads, you consciously see, hear, taste, smell, and touch what is right here, right now, you automatically disconnect guilt and worry neurons. That allows you to turn on new neurons of acceptance of what is, not what you hope is true, but what is going on right now in this moment in your life.

. . . . .

Am I Willing to be Totally Honest with Myself?

Therapists are trained not to believe everything their clients tell them, nor to doubt everything either. That's a good thing, for as any therapist can tell you, honesty is a hard commodity to come by when clients initially enter therapy, and the same can be true when they begin work with a coach. Some want to impress the "authority" figure. Some are so used to putting on a false front that they can't stop even in the presence of someone who can help them learn to live more authentically. Others want to deflect any responsibility for their situation onto others because in the past they've been humiliated or punished excessively when they did something wrong. Then there are those who, unfortunately, were not raised to be honest, having been allowed to get by with whatever they could. Still others deny their negative qualities (and even their good ones) because they genuinely do not see them, for it can take time to recognize what is often called "our shadow side," both positive and negative.

Alcoholics and drug abusers are great at lying to themselves, and to others. In fact, one of the major reasons some people have difficulty in staying with any alcohol or drug recovery program is that honesty is required if it's going to work, and addicts don't have much experience in that arena. They've become very clever at hiding the truth.

If you want your life to change, telling the truth about yourself is the best policy, even if it's hard to do. And if you think others won't approve of how you answer the questions in this book, just remember that there isn't any authority, parent, child, boss, or friend looking over your shoulder and giving you a sincerity test here. You get to choose which questions you will answer. You are the only one who needs to know how you've answered them. There is no one to impress, or disappoint, but yourself.

ASK YOURSELF ABOUT HONESTY

When is it most difficult for me to be honest? Why?

When is it easiest for me to tell the truth? Why?

So the only thing to do is to be totally, completely honest with yourself. It is the equivalent of opening your backpack and looking at *whatever* you find there. If you do this with an open mind, you'll not waste your time, energy and, if you're seeing a therapist or coach, money. The only person whose opinion about "who you are" really matters is you. Give your opinions with honesty and appreciation for all the good things you've accomplished and the lessons you've learned.

**YOUR LIFE STORY
IN THREE SENTENCES**

*Imagine you are asked to write the story of
your life in three chapters titled:*

- *What Has Happened To Me Up Until
Now?*
- *What Is Happening Right Now?*
- *What Do I Expect Will Happen In The
Future?*

*What would be the first sentence you would
write for each of these chapters?*

What Story Do I Most Like to Tell About My Life?

Every story we tell about ourselves is chosen for a particular purpose. We may tell a story so that in the telling of it we can make sense of what is happening in our corner of the world (or in the whole uncertain world in which we find ourselves today). Often in the beginning of the story we may not know how we'll feel by the end because we're listening to ourselves and figuring it out as we go along. In most stories, however, we are clear about what it is we believe about ourselves — and we want others to see us as we see ourselves.

Our egos love to share stories based on everything we carry in our backpack. Some of us enjoy telling stores of what we have accomplished. Our listeners may be impressed with how confident we seem. Others of us, even though we may not be quite sure of ourselves, can pull off a good story to make it appear that we've got our act together. It is through our stories that others see us as a loser or a winner, as secure or lacking self-confidence, as generous or stingy.

A story of past injustice is told to let others know how

wronged we were, how we were a victim of cruel circumstances, and how our response was the only logical thing to do. As we tell our story, we let others know — through our tone of voice, the words we choose, our gestures and our posture — the parts of the story we want them to remember.

Recently we had dinner with a highly successful businessman who told one fantastic story after the other about his exploits. Each of them was interesting, in and of itself. As the centerpiece for conversation with a table of ten, however, it was too much. If the purpose of his stories was to let us know he was successful, he succeeded. But if the purpose was to connect more closely with us, it didn't work. On the ride home we decided that he was what one might call "a little full of himself." I wondered why he felt it important for us to know so much about him. Perhaps he was more insecure than he wanted his stories to convey.

Stretching the Truth

Since there are so many stories that reflect lives that are more colorful than the ones we live, we may be tempted to insert into our stories experiences that never happened. There are hundreds, if not thousands, of books (and countless résumés) that present the author's life as though he or she is more brilliant, more lucky, more creative, and more educated than he or she actually is.

It is not surprising story-tellers view their lives as thin and inconsequential when viewed in comparison to stories they hear on TV and see in the movies. If we could look beyond the spin of even the most sterling of our idols, however, we might discover that the story we hear is not really the *whole* story. For example, *In the Shadow of Fame: A Memoir by the Daughter of Erik H. Erikson* illustrates how the private life of a very famous person was far from the picture he wanted us to see.

Without turning her famous psychoanalyst father — who extended Freud's stages of development to encompass the entire life span and who was highly regarded as an icon of childhood development theory — into a wicked father, Sue Erikson Bloland shares the reality of his life. This included the birth of a son with Down Syndrome who was institutionalized and never spoken of in the family or in public, and a work-obsessed father whose family life was designed to revolve around him. He was effective in presenting his life, but only as long as he controlled the telling of it.

Family Myths

One of the most interesting forms of story-telling is the story a family tells about a member of the family, or perhaps an event, that demonstrates how the family responds to triumphs and traumas. We all have such stories tucked away in our backpacks. They let others know that "our" family is special in some particular way. These stories are repeated over the years until everyone gets the point: The qualities of the people in our story are significant characteristics of our family! The story doesn't necessarily have to be true, which is why it is called a family "myth," but it does need to express an emotional lesson for members of the family.

Thus, one family may conclude that Grandma's shrewd decision to withdraw money from the stock market in August of 1929, two months before the market crashed and the Great Depression began, means she was clever. When this story is told, there is a clear implication that women in the family are astute and shrewd. The truth may be that she had merely cashed out her stocks to buy a farm and the timing just *happened* to be convenient.

In another family, stories are told each time something un-fortunate happens, making the case that their family always has "bad luck." Consequently, the members of that family don't have to look for, or acknowledge, the part their poor choices play in undesired outcomes. Any evidence that they, themselves, may contribute to what happens to them is ignored in favor of an interpretation in which "bad luck" is responsible.

Stories That Heal

Too often, people must experience greater tragedy than the ordinary misfortunes that come into every life. In these cases, it is often in the telling of the tragedy that victims are released from the pain and paralysis of the past.

An example of this was the basis of a riveting play titled, *I Have Before Me a Remarkable Document Given to Me by a Young Lady from Rwanda,* by Sonja Linden. The play grew out of the story of a young woman from Rwanda who lost almost her entire family in the slaughter of hundreds of thousands of Tutsis by the Hutus in the 1990s. What started out as the writing of her family's experience of genocide, so that people would not forget what happened, became, in addition, an act of healing.

For two-and-a-half years she had worked on her book in the refugee camp, wrestling day after day with her enormously painful story, often tearing up the previous day's work at five o'clock in the morning when she started her daily writing. Even while she was immersed in the process of writing her book, however, she recognized its therapeutic value and said that writing helped her take the pain "away from my heart." Consequently, she discovered that through telling her story she came to feel "clean" and her nightmares and headaches ceased. As I watched the play and heard her horrendous tale, my heart cried for her and I will not forget her family, or the suffering of her people, which was, of course, the original purpose of writing her story.

FILL-IN-THE-BLANKS FOR
A LITTLE SELF-ANALYSIS

I am _____
    [STATE HOW YOU SEE YOURSELF]
because _____
    [REASON YOU VIEW YOURSELF THAT WAY]

I am _____
    [STATE HOW YOU SEE YOURSELF]
because _____
    [REASON YOU VIEW YOURSELF THAT WAY]

I am _____
    [STATE HOW YOU SEE YOURSELF]
because _____
    [REASON YOU VIEW YOURSELF THAT WAY]

Continue until you've written every description about yourself that you can think of.

It is through the telling and retelling of a tragedy that we can begin to work through the awful memories of that event. As we gradually become freed from the terror, shame, confusion, and fear of an experience, we will tell the story with different inflections, different gestures, different words. We may think of these stories as "dynamic" because, through telling them over and over again, we come to a new understanding of whatever it was that happened long ago. Over time, we develop maturity and have a different viewpoint from which to comprehend what happened back then. So our story shifts.

Moving Into a New Story

On the other hand, "static" stories carry the same emotional overtones every time they are told. The story-teller uses the same gestures, the same words and the same expressions. It doesn't matter whether the story is positive or negative, it has "crystallized" into a form that shelters the ego and prevents the person from having to explore the original situation from a different perspective. The more complex and convoluted the story is, the more frequently it retains its original flavor.

I believe that one of the reasons this happens is that stories can be enchanting not only for the listener, but for the one telling the story as well. Consequently, if told with enthusiasm, we are fascinated by our own experience. If our audience seems receptive and offers sympathy or praise, we tell our story to others with the same inflections and the same pauses for sighs and laughter. After awhile, however, when we've repeated the story over and over and over again, we may notice that we're not as interested (nor is our audience) as we were the first few times we told it. We might then consider whether we are caught in the drama of our story, or whether we are still exploring what the experience means to us.

We like old stories, of course, provided they aren't repeated *too* frequently. They have a familiar, comfortable ring to them. But life continually changes, taking twists and turns we hadn't expected. So it's valuable to remember that there are good things to come even when life hasn't been so great lately, and there are likely to be some rough times ahead even though today everything is absolutely fine.

Whenever we act as though we can control the ending of our story, I'm reminded of something Gilda Radner said

ASK YOURSELF ABOUT A STORY YOU LIKE TO TELL

The last time I told someone about an incident in my childhood, was it different than it had been when I first told that story?

If so, why? If not, why not?

after she was diagnosed with cervical cancer:

> *I wanted a perfect ending. Now I've learned, the hard way, that some poems don't rhyme, and some stories don't have a clear beginning, middle, and end. Life is about not knowing, having to change, taking the moment and making the best of it, without knowing what's going to happen next. Delicious Ambiguity.*

May the questions in this book bring you "delicious ambiguity." May they help you move out of your present comfort zone, and into an embrace of the possibility that your life doesn't have to be perfect for you to notice the potential for pleasure inherent in every day. If nothing else, the questions can help you gain courage to tell your stories straight up, full of honesty, humor, and love.

It is good to remember that changing our lives is often a matter of learning how to change the way we tell our stories, and listening to the stories of others with an open heart.

. . . . .

What Do I Like About Me and My Life?

There may be people, like the man who monopolized the dinner conversation, who have no trouble telling us what's good about them. Then there are others who couldn't say something nice about themselves if their life depended on it.

Most of us are probably somewhere in the middle. We may consider ourselves better than average in many areas (studies show this is true for the majority of people). But we are not generally blind to our flaws (although studies also show that the average person believes he or she has fewer of them than others). The problem is that when we do notice our imperfections, we can too often focus them, on the cracks in

33

our relationships, on the body image that doesn't match the model's, on the aches and pains that are part of every life. When we're obsessed with imperfection, it's difficult not only to accept, but to appreciate and actually like ourselves very much.

If we can't appreciate what is good about us and our lives, and if we can't keep our problems in perspective, we become like my son the day he came home from a school field trip to the science museum. I asked him how his day went. "Bad," he replied. "Bad?," I echoed. "Were the exhibits not what you thought they would be?" "No, they were good." "Was the bus ride bad?" "No, that was okay." After a long question-and-answer period, I discovered he didn't like the sandwich I packed for his lunch!

ASK YOURSELF ABOUT YOUR SKILLS

What do I wish I could learn to do?

Am I willing to learn how to do it?

What could I accomplish if I had those skills?

Mistakes are evidence we're human, as Tim, Sue, and Pat illustrate. At the holiday office party Tim forgot the name of a high-level manager, someone he wanted to impress, just as he started to introduce him to his spouse. Sue spilled coffee on a report twenty minutes before she was to present it to an important client. Pat unconsciously tossed her daughter's favorite shirt into the dryer, where it shrank.

Any of those mistakes can have consequences one would rather not deal with. Tim's boss is not impressed with his memory. Sue may lose a client. Pat's daughter is convinced her mother doesn't care about her things. Nevertheless, as the common phrase goes, to err is human. Such events are part of life.

However, if we constantly kick ourselves for not living up to our expectations, or what we believe are the expectations others have of us, we'll miss a lot of pleasure. If we skip over our good qualities and only see fodder for a long self-improvement project, an arduous journey of seeking perfection lies ahead of us. [In CHAPTER TWO and in the APPENDIX you'll find additional comments about perfectionism, which I can tell you from personal experience can make your life more difficult than it needs to be.]

The fact is that we often fail to give ourselves credit for the ordinary things we do without effort. For example, do you find it easy to talk with strangers? Some people are scared to death of starting a conversation with someone they haven't known for years. Do you know how to sew? Some people can't even sew on a button. Do you enjoy reading novels? Your life is richer for it. Do you get up and run every morning? Your life is healthier because of it. Do you work at a homeless shelter? The world is better for it.

The world needs all the skills, talents and gifts you have to give, no matter how insignificant they may seem.

Self-esteem is More Than Liking Yourself

If you don't easily acknowledge your talents, you may be accused of not having "self-esteem." Let's see whether that is really so. You see, one of the problems in determining whether one has "self-esteem" arises from the frequent misuse of the term. Often people use it to mean someone "likes" himself or herself. On the surface of it, that would seem desirable. But too high of regard for oneself can result in narcissism, conceit, arrogance, superiority, and intolerance of the frailties of others.

In my experience, and I imagine in yours, I've known people

who don't think positively about themselves, yet perform nobly both in the face of great challenge and in the drudgery and weariness of daily responsibilities. Conversely, convicted felons can feel quite proud of themselves. Those who commit crimes and *don't* get caught can feel twice as proud for having eluded capture! So if someone views his self-esteem as a feel-good phenomena, it does not necessarily mean he contributes to a more productive society.

That is why I like the definition of self-esteem used by The National Association of Self-esteem: "The experience of being capable of meeting life's challenges and being worthy of happiness."

In answering the questions in this chapter I hope you will search out every corner of your wonderful life and find many things to appreciate and celebrate. There will be plenty of time later to explore what in your life you would like to be different than it is today.

. . . . .

Am I Following My Dreams or Someone Else's?

Imagine that your paycheck doesn't stretch as far as it once did, the town where you live is getting a bit overcrowded, and you're itching to live someplace else. Fortunately, someone tells you about a country far across the sea to the west, where the cost of living is extremely low. There's nothing particularly attractive about that place, but you decide it will suit you fine. So you buy a small sailboat (you've always wanted to have one), load it with provisions, and set your compass for due west.

The second day out, you notice another boat sailing in your direction. As it pulls alongside, you tell the captain where you're going. "Well," he says, "I've been there and I

36

admit it's a bit less expensive than some other countries, but the scenery is dull and gray as rock. Now, me, I like my scenery to be more lively and if you do, too, then you'd love a country that lies far to the north." Since you appreciate beauty, you convince yourself that you could learn to be a bit tighter with your money, that economy isn't all that important, and so change your compass to due north.

After sailing for a few days, you see a ship coming toward you. As you exchange greetings with the crew, you learn about yet another land, far to the south, where the climate is "absolutely wonderful all year long." It is true, they tell you, that the cities are a bit overcrowded, but the perfect weather more than makes up for it. Afraid that long winters in the north won't be to your liking after all, and that it really wasn't so bad living in a busy city, you decide that comfortable weather is an important criteria for choosing a place to live. Once again you reset you compass and off you head for the south.

> ### ASK YOURSELF ABOUT YOUR DREAMS
>
> What am I doing today because someone else wants me to do it, even though in my heart I know it is not right for me?
>
> What makes it easy for me to defer my dreams to the wishes of others?

We could continue this metaphor (which is similar to the metaphor about your "backpack") endlessly, for there are always people who have opinions on what makes a place desirable. Consequently, if you can't decide the standards that are most important to you — and if you don't stick with them — you'll use up all your provisions and never arrive at any destination.

Unfortunately, many people allow their lives to shift from goal to goal in just this way, basing their decisions on what others tell them they *should* do. While they may have a general idea of what they like and dislike, they haven't fully explored what is most important to them. Consequently, their compass never points in the direction that fulfills their personal needs. They're doomed to play the game of life under someone else's rules.

It's understandable that we can be confused about what is best for us. Every day we're bombarded by advertising, news commentators and editorials, to say nothing of friends and family who eagerly give us their views on every topic under the sun. All of them want us to either buy their product, donate to their cause, or believe in their opinions.

Except for out-and-out charlatans, advice-givers sincerely believe that our lives will be better if we follow their advice. But whether that would be wise or foolish, we cannot possibly set our compasses to go in all those directions at the same time. Yet because life offers us many more choices today than we've ever had, the in-what-direction-should-I-set-my-compass problem is increasingly common.

How can you know your purpose in life and the best setting for your personal compass? Return again to "the room with a view." That is one of the best ways to discover your purpose in life — or rediscover a purpose you previously held that has become neglected and forgotten.

The more you listen to your heart and follow the dreams of your true self, the less energy you'll spend trying to follow someone else's dreams. The more you look carefully at what you love to do, but have perhaps neglected, the more easily you can turn your ship in a direction that gives your life meaning. The more you choose to live consciously day-to-day, the more you will discover that your purpose in life will unfold much as a caterpillar gradually emerges from a chrysalis into a butterfly.

If you want to change your life, reflect on these questions from CHAPTER TWO:

- *Who am I today?*

- *Am I willing to be totally honest with myself?*

- *What story do I most like to tell about my life? Why?*

- *What do I like about me and my life? Why?*

- *Am I following my dreams or someone else's? Why?*

CHAPTER THREE

How Has My Past Influenced My Life Today?

Whether our family consisted of a mother and father, a single parent, a mother and three step-fathers or three step-mothers and one father, two moms or two dads, grandparents who took over the parenting role, foster parents, a commune in the woods, or any other combination of people who take on the responsibility of raising children, it was within that family that we learned our first lessons about goal-setting and the possibility for change.

Within strong and well-functioning families children are able to learn that they have the ability to make wise choices and to be responsible for the consequences of their choices. They learn that striving and failing is part of the human condition and that we all fail at one time or another.

These positive lessons begin very early. In fact, they begin in the first three years if a mother, or other significant caregiver, is attuned to the child's emotional states and responds appropriately. From those early experiences, and other positive relationships, will come a strong sense of self, a belief that he can care for himself, the freedom and courage of self-confidence, and the ability to choose what is best for him and others. All of these strengths, and more, are possible because the child's brain is developing a network of neuronal connections that support self-awareness and self-determination. These positive pathways are developed to a large degree through the interaction of caregivers and child. Thus our sense of self is developed through our connection with others. Nature *needs* nurture.

ASK YOURSELF HOW YOUR MOTHER INFLUENCED YOUR DECISIONS

- What did (does) my mother hope I would (will) be?
- How did (does) my mother encourage me to make my own choices?
- What did (does) my mother say when she wanted (wants) to praise me?
- What did (does) my mother say when she wanted (wants) to criticize me?
- What did (does) my mother say about success?
- What did (does) my mother say about failure?
- What did (does) my mother say about trying to do my best?
- If I don't remember what my mother said, what do I think she might have said?
- How do I let the need for my mother's approval still influence my decisions and goal-setting?

What Effect as My Family Had On My Ability to Achieve My Goals?

Earlier I mentioned family myths when discussing the importance of stories families tell themselves. There are two other ways in which each generation passes on to the next generation concepts about success and failure, winning and losing, trying and failing.

The first are family rules. These are the "unwritten laws" of the family and they have great power to create, maintain,

ASK YOURSELF HOW YOUR FATHER INFLUENCED YOUR DECISIONS

- What did (does) my father hope I would (will) be?
- How did (does) my father encourage me to make my own choices?
- What did (does) my father say when he wanted (wants) to praise me?
- What did (does) my father say when he wanted (wants) to criticize me?
- What did (does) my father say about success?
- What did (does) my father say about failure?
- What did (does) my father say about trying to do my best?
- If I don't remember what my father said, what do I think he might have said?
- How do I let the need for my father's approval still influence my decisions and goal-setting?

and control the life of every family. Some of the rules are formal, out in the open for all to see, and everyone is conscious of what is required. However, the majority of family rules are informal, hidden, and unconscious, which makes their emotional significance even more potent.

Similar to powerful family rules, every family has rituals that reinforce those rules and bind the family as a unit. These rituals demonstrate in concrete ways how we are to respond to events of birth and death, money and work, love and lifestyle.

As discussed in CHAPTER ONE, we carry with us rituals, rules, myths, traditions, beliefs, etc. that may no longer be appropriate for our life today, but they are deeply buried in the psyche (that is, our old backpack).

When children grow up, leave the nest and fly off on their own, they bring with them concepts about choices and goal-setting that they've absorbed from the rules, rituals and myths that were an integral part of the old nest. Yet what we learned back then may not be appropriate for the new nest we create after leaving home. The difficulty arises when deciding which traditions and concepts are valuable to keep and which need to be discarded so that we can make appropriate choices for the future.

It isn't necessary to delve deeply into your past in order to solve problems in the present. You don't have to have a cathartic experience in reliving old wounds in order to function well today. But it certainly helps to understand which of your family rules, rituals and myths encouraged success and which are ones that prevented you from choosing wisely.

. . . . .

What Have My Experiences Taught Me About Choosing and Reaching Goals?

Your parents aren't the only ones who've influenced your ability to be successful. You've played a significant role as well. It's called "experience." Or perhaps it might more appropriately be called the "experiments" in life.

You see, before something happens, you don't know how you will experience that event. You can certainly make a calculated guess based on past experiences. For example, you may choose to watch the sequel of a movie because you greatly enjoyed the first one. But you can't count on the second being as good, can you? It's an experiment. It may be great fun, maybe even better than the first movie, but it's no sure bet.

When you deliberately select one experience rather than another, you place yourself in the role of experimenter. You are making a hypothesis that one choice will cause you to experience an event one way and another choice will provide another experience. After you have finished the experience, you discover how your "experiment" turned out.

> **ASK YOURSELF ABOUT CHOICES**
>
> What choice out of all the thousands of choices I've made has most impacted my life? Why?
>
> What choice do I most regret? Why?

Think of how different your life has been because you chose the college you did or decided not to go to college at all, because you joined the debate team instead of the water polo team, because you married Barbara instead of Jane or Bill instead of Jim, because you decided to practice piano or stopped lessons because they were boring. The experiences (the experiments) you've had that result from these choices can be either positive, negative or somewhere in-between. All of them influence how you will make choices in the future.

When we are placed in situations we don't choose to have, we still have a choice in how we will respond to them. Consider how great trauma and significant loss can eventually turn into new patterns of behavior. As hard as it may appear when trauma first hits, by the time you've been dragged, often kicking, screaming, and gnashing your teeth, into new circumstances without the object you lost — be it spouse, house, job, health, dream, or belief in a fact that proves untrue — you may discover that you are a different, and better, person for it. It may be that you won't be any different after the upheaval in your life than you were before, yet many people are transformed by their greatest setbacks and challenges.

Fortunately, we also learn life's lessons from pleasant experiences. When you are laughing and having a good time with people you love, you mentally put a check-mark in your list of events you want to choose again. Exploring your past experiences, and the lessons they offer, can make you more aware of how you might be holding yourself back from pursuing a goal that will give you an opportunity to have more experiences on which to build a new you, or at least an improved version.

Through your relationships, schooling, work, church, recreation, and social organizations you develop skills that allow you to negotiate, persuade, analyze, and teach. All of these skills, especially if grounded in a love of learning, provide a growing opportunity for experiences that make each new goal more possible to achieve.

. . . . .

How Have My Values and My Faith Influenced My Choices in Life?

We are born utterly dependent on others not only for physical sustenance, but for guidance in how the world works and how we should live. That's why we count on our parents, having been around a lot longer than we have, to show us the world, limited though their view might be.

As I said earlier, when we're children we don't question these core beliefs. Then the teen years come along and it's open season on our parents' standards! What do parents know anyway? They were teenagers eons ago! They don't understand the pressures we're under today!

I realize, of course, that teens with "helicopter parents" who hover over every decision they make may enjoy having parents navigate for them through high school and even college. But the launching stage is a time when children need to move from dependence to independence to interdependence, when the task of that age is to discover the values they want to follow. If parents do their job well enough, their strong values almost certainly rub off on their children. They will have given them a values compass that can guide them through many conflicts and challenges.

> **ASK YOURSELF ABOUT YOUR VALUES AND YOUR DECISIONS**
>
> When I am about to make a decision at work or in a relationship, do I stop to think consciously about how the beliefs I claim to hold will affect my decision and, thus, my actions?

If you were raised in a religion that does not tolerate dissent or allow questions, you may not consider any choice valid that lies beyond the narrow parameters you have been allowed to experience. On the other hand, if your

47

parents believed that all ideas have equal value, everything is relative, and there are no firm rights and wrongs, you may not have a strong values compass against which you can evaluate your choices.

Whether extremely narrow or extremely broad, religious beliefs don't grow deep tap roots if they are not experienced wholeheartedly, but merely swallowed whole because our parents tell us what to believe. One day the ideas that once were comforting will no longer seem to apply to our lives. Later we may find that going to church, temple or mosque can be just one more thing in a schedule that already has too many commitments clamoring for attention.

Then, gradually, the idea of following the dictates of a religious dogma becomes less and less attractive. Our faith can vanish in a culture that places power, beauty and appearance above commitment to ideals, some of which require genuine sacrifice. And religious beliefs may not be attractive when extreme fundamentalists, of every stripe, give religion a bad name.

Nevertheless, whether we continue to practice the religion in which we grew up, find another faith to follow, decide to give up entirely on religion, or follow spiritual practices that may be foreign to our parents, each of us chooses the values and standards we hold up as an ideal.

We may claim that we don't decide which values and beliefs are the right ones and believe we are merely following the teaching of someone who speaks "the truth." The reality is that we are the ones who decide who will be our guide and which, out of dozens, if not hundreds, of interpretations of scripture, or of plain old principles for moral and ethical living, is the correct one.

In any case, to the extent that our faith and our values

influence our choices and therefore our actions, it is important to notice whether we live what we say we believe, or only give lip service to an ideal.

. . . . .

How Have I Allowed Emotions To Get in the Way of Reaching My Goals?

Emotions can trip you up at the most inconvenient times, and can certainly place stumbling blocks on the road to change.

You're pleasantly going about your business (convinced you're making progress on an important step on the way to success) when someone does or says something and suddenly your stomach churns . . . your head pounds . . . you get extremely angry . . . or you're swept with an overwhelming sense of incompetence and feel like a total jerk. It doesn't matter that you know your reaction is way out of proportion to what just occurred. What does matter is that you don't know how to stop yourself. Why can't you take the advice of others when they tell you, "Just don't let it bother you"?

All of us are overly sensitive to some topics and feel insecure about ourselves in one way or another. When someone puts us down with a thoughtless comment, when a superior brusquely demands we redo a project we thought was already quite good, when a driver cuts us off on the highway, we can be overwhelmed by our emotions — rather than simply telling ourselves that these people could use some lessons in tact and kindness.

To explain how I experience this phenomena, and how I see it in other people, I will give you another metaphor. I think that when this happens it's almost as though something physically prevents us from reacting any other way, like a helpless piece of Velcro® that can't resist getting hooked by the barbs on another piece of Velcro®.

That is why I call this very human dynamic the "Velcro® Syndrome." It is created from our blind spots, from excessive self-criticism, from a sense of insecurity or superiority, from strongly held beliefs, and from the many unpolished parts of our personalities. Consequently, when our rough spots get hooked by the rough places in the personalities of our bosses, neighbors, friends, siblings, parents and children, we get pulled off-balance. Unfortunately, because we're as flawed as the next person, we also say and do things that unintentionally offend others and pull them off-balance.

On the other hand, there is a characteristic of this material which is important to remember. A very, very small piece of it will stick to another piece of any size. Consequently, no matter what your size of Velcro® may be, there's a good chance it will get hooked by another person. Fortunately, however, the smaller your piece, the easier it is to disengage yourself after you're caught, even if the *other* person's piece is extremely large. Therein lies the possibility that you can extricate yourself from Velcro® moments.

Learning to Master Fear

There are a number of emotions that can create the Velcro® Syndrome. The most common, though, is an emotion that has an inordinate capacity to interfere with our intention to change. Fear. When fear is your master, it controls you in many ways, particularly when you want your life to change in a fairly significant way.

When fear is your master, you bring the future into the present.
When you master fear, you accept the future only
when it actually arrives.

When fear is your master, you forget that you can learn to solve new problems.
When you master fear, you remember how good it

feels to bring your skills into new situations.

When fear is your master, you believe you have to face life's challenges all by yourself.

> When you master fear, you remember the many times when you've expressed your feelings and your needs clearly and have been supported by others.

When fear is your master, you stop trying because you might make a mistake.

> When you master fear, you gain strength from the many times you've made a mistake, forgiven yourself, learned from it, and moved on.

When fear is your master, you focus on the separate details of life, judging one thing as good and another as bad, with a particular emphasis on the bad, unable to see life as a whole.

> When you master fear, you remember the times that you have transcended your sense of separateness, times when you experienced the ordinary, individual details of life as a whole, when you felt a connection with the essence of life.

Finally, when fear, a very serious emotion, is your master, you ignore the pleasures that life offers.

> When you master fear, you live in each moment as it happens, discovering that you can't be overwhelmed by what *may* — or *may not* — happen in the future because you're fully focused on the present.

Remembering Your Ability to Manage Emotions

If you give careful consideration to the questions in the box on the next page, you will realize that negative emotions have not always prevented you from achieving success. You *have had* the ability to stay in charge when strong emotions have tried to focus all your attention on their agenda for your life. So when you start to berate yourself for not being cool, calm, and collected all the time, remember that you have emotional strengths. The thing to explore is *how* you have done that and what those experiences have taught you. Then, when strong emotions, from anger to fear and jealousy to depression, attempt to prevent you from reaching the goals you want, you can look into your backpack and remember the tools you've successfully used in the past.

Also, as you answer the questions in this book and notice your strengths as well as the areas in which you need to grow, you will gradually decrease your Velcro® and gain confidence in managing your emotions because emotional reactions have their roots in beliefs and unexplored beliefs and unfinished business.

ASK YOURSELF ABOUT EMOTIONS

- How have I managed to control my fear when I needed to do something I was afraid of doing?

- How have I managed to control my anger when I needed to do something and was angry?

- How have I managed my sadness when it threatened to engulf me in pain and prevent me from moving forward?

- How have I managed my guilt when it caught me in a spiral of self-criticism and tried to keep me tied to the past?

- How have I managed my jealousy when it threatened to separate me from satisfying relationships?

Does Perfectionism Keep Me From Achieving My Goals Comfortably?

Not everyone, thank goodness, is a perfectionist. But as a recovering perfectionist, I know how perfectionism can make the achievement of goals more difficult than it needs to be. So let's begin to explore this personality trait by using my definition of perfectionism:

> *A perfectionist is one who strives to reach very high standards and is displeased by anything that does not meet those standards. However, when perfectionists are asked whether they define themselves as perfectionists, the answer is almost always, "No, I'm not. I'm just trying to do my best and meet the standards that are expected of me."*

What is the consequence of this personality characteristic? For starters, in a world where the consistent achievement of high standards is not the norm, perfectionists feel displeased much of the time!

Self-critical, judgmental of others, and opinionated, they often find it hard to see the other person's point of view, although they may be quite pleasant and courteous in their relationships. However, the distance between themselves and others is exacerbated because they tend to feel either "omnipotent" or "impotent."

You see, perfectionists pretty much only feel good about themselves when they do something as well as it can possibly be done (and then some). An "A+" is evidence they are not ordinary mortals. They experience this as "omnipotence" (or something that comes very close to that feeling), even though they wouldn't acknowledge it. On the other hand, what happens when they fail, which, being human, they are bound to do? Then they feel "impotent," guilty, and shamed.

Unfortunately, their shame turns into anger, which is often suppressed or denied, though others may feel the effects of it.

This anger comes from constantly assuming the other person — spouse, teacher, parent, sibling, friend, boss, or even children (though on second thought, we generally don't have to guess whether our kids think we live up to their expectations) — believes the perfectionist didn't do what he or she was "supposed" to do, or didn't do it well enough. In actual fact, the person may have done *exactly* what another person wanted (or would have been satisfied to accept) long before the perfectionist finally gets around to finishing a project.

To the average person it would seem only reasonable to check with others to see what they really want from us. But from the perspective of a perfectionist, this would be a sign of weakness and indicate he or she hadn't understood the instructions, mind-reading being one of the skills perfectionists think they "ought" to have. Since they need the approval of others so badly, they're not willing to confront the other person and learn whether they've guessed correctly. So they put on a cheerful face, yet shudder in fear they won't be liked!

Then there is the control-oriented characteristic of perfectionists. When they are put into a position where someone else is supposed to be in charge but is doing a poor job of it, they find the situation distressing. In large part, this is because perfectionists not only have high standards they set for themselves, they expect others to meet high standards.

At the same time, they're ambivalent about making decisions. If they were to make a decision that wasn't to everyone's satisfaction, they will experience the shame of believing others will criticize their ability to make decisions. So they put off choices until the last possible moment, trying to avoid the possibility that they would choose wrong!

I hope the picture I've tried to paint of perfectionists shows them as complex people trying to balance many conflicting pressures in their efforts to get through life without having others know they aren't handling things as perfectly as they "should."

Since the core of their inner dynamics is closely tied to shame, an emotion that causes the person not only to feel they might disappoint someone else but that they are, at their core, bad in some way. This deep-seated belief can require a lot of work to ease the fear of disappointing someone (including themselves), but if your personality style happens to be that of a perfectionist, I want you to know that recovery is possible. Life *can be* lived with less pressure, and goals more easily achieved, when you become a recovering perfectionist. [The APPENDIX offers you a chance to explore whether you have perfectionist tendencies and CHAPTER FIVE shows you how to counter perfectionism with acceptance.]

If you want to change your life, reflect on these questions from CHAPTER THREE:

- *How has my past influenced my life today?*

- *What effect has my family had on my ability to achieve my goals? Why do I believe that is so?*

- *What have my experiences taught me about choosing and reaching goals?*

- *How have my values and my faith influenced my choices in life?*

- *How have I allowed emotions to get in the way of reaching my goals?*

- *Does perfectionism keep me from achieving my goals comfortably?*

CHAPTER FOUR

How Do I Want My Life to Be Different?

I talked about a "call to action" in CHAPTER ONE and said that I would use the story of a young man's heroic journey to explain the process of change, for the stages he moves through as he reaches his full potential have been a central feature of literature and theatre for centuries. Now is a good time to meet him, in the first stage of his journey.

The Heroic Journey

STAGE ONE

Our story begins in a small town in the middle of the Middle Ages. A young man named Roger lives with his family above the wool and fabric store owned by his father. His parents and five younger siblings are comfortable in their middle-class lifestyle and it has always been assumed that, being the oldest son, he will inherit his father's business.

Our potential hero is not so sure. For several years he's been thinking about the deaths of his three

---

younger brothers. In each case there was a simple infection or illness and the local healer was called. She applied potions and offered herbal teas, but none of her efforts was enough to prevent rapid deterioration of his brother's condition.

This healer is an old woman who claims to have learned everything from her mother and her grandmother, but it seems to Roger that her learning is limited. Otherwise, why couldn't she have saved his brothers? His brothers hadn't appeared to be terribly sick when the old woman first came to the house, but she had an air about her of authority and spoke of mysterious potions known only by her. Now he wonders whether someone, somewhere, knows more.

Then one hot day when Roger is getting a drink from the town well, a stranger rides up and introduces himself, saying, "I'm George Eadric and I sell herbs. I'm looking for a healer who might be interested in buying some." When Roger tells him where to find her, he adds that he doesn't think much of her healing abilities. Then, out of curiosity, he asks how someone can become a really good healer using herbs.

Before he knows it, he has not only learned there is a healer in a town a long way away with a reputation of having excellent knowledge about herbs—he realizes that what he wants to do more than anything in the world is to become a better healer than the one his family uses. That would be much more exciting for him than selling fabrics and overseeing wool-carding.

Like heroes who've gone before him, and those who will come after, every potential hero needs someone, or some circumstance, that will challenge, nudge, confront, inspire, and dare him to go beyond the edge of his ordinary existence. That's the role that George plays in this story. By giving Roger information he didn't have before, he sets in motion the opportunity for Roger to begin a wonderful journey, though it isn't apparent in the beginning. All the young man realizes at the time is that he has heard the call and is ready to respond, even though he knows nothing of what awaits him.

That night Roger tells his father that he plans to study herbology. The argument that follows is about what you might expect in the circumstances. While his father understands Roger was upset by his brothers' deaths, he doesn't believe his son could learn any more than the old healer. But the next morning, when his father has gone off to check on the purchase of wool from a local farmer, Roger tells his mother that the only path for him is learning about herbs. Understanding the motivation for his decision, she packs a bag with food and a little money to get him started, telling him she looks forward to his return.

To leave his village, Roger has to go through a gate in the wall that separates the safety of his familiar surroundings from land outside, what some call the "zone unknown." When he reaches the gate, there is a guardian with keys jangling from his belt who questions him, "Why do you want me to unlock the gate for you? Why do you want to leave the sanctuary of home and hearth and set out into the wild unknown? Don't you know that you could be set upon by robbers and vicious animals could devour you?"

TO BE CONTINUED

I could have chosen a young woman for this adventure, of course, but during the time in which this story takes place few young women would have been able to set out on the adventure that Roger has. Nevertheless, I must emphasize that those who step out into the unknown, overcome great obstacles, and reach a distant goal can be a member of either sex. Also, remember that such adventures can happen at any age, whether the person is very young, going through a mid-life crisis, or finding an opportunity for adventure in the later years of life.

Now that you've read the first stage of Roger's journey, you are ready to look at what might be *your* call to action. Changing careers. Moving to a different town to be with your boyfriend. Learning a new language. Applying to graduate school. Losing weight. Asking someone to marry you. Getting a divorce. Stopping smoking. Taking action to no longer abuse drugs and alcohol. Writing a historical novel. Studying ceramics. Entering the ministry. Or a thousand other dreams we humans have dreamed for centuries.

ASK YOURSELF IF NOW IS THE TIME FOR CHANGE

If what I want to change about my life is the same, or similar, to something I've wanted for a long time, what makes it more pressing today than in the past?

Before you decide you will do any of those things, whether it's something you've thought about for a long time or something that's only recently caught your interest, accomplishing your goal can be tough-going. If it weren't, you would probably have done it long ago. So I want to emphasize that you will be able to say "no" to what you might, at this time, think is your call to action. Perhaps what you want to change in your life is not something that needs changing right now and you need to stay in your comfort zone a bit longer. You can decide that later.

As you will discover when going through the questions in this book, for you to be successful when you step through the gate to your future, you must be serious about where you want to go, and why.

What is My Call to Action?

If something or someone is pushing or pulling you toward change, or if you feel an increasing level of physical or emotional discomfort you haven't felt before, now is the time to explore what lies behind your interest in changing your life.

You may be very clear about what it is that needs more than a minor adjustment in your life. However, if it seems as though nothing is going right in your life and many things demand your attention, I suggest you rank the problems so you don't feel overwhelmed.

Ask yourself, "How much do I want to improve my finances, career, education, health, emotional well-being, spiritual practice and religious faith, or my relationship with a significant other or with my children?" Then use a scale of "1" to "10" to discover what specific area of your life needs attention first. Let "1" represent something that is of very low importance for you at this time and "10" means there is a pressing need for improvement.

What if you have more than one thing in your life to which you give a high rank? Then I recommend you take a page from the life of Ben Franklin. You see, early in our country's history, when Ben Franklin was a young man, it seems that a Quaker came to him one day and said something to the effect that, "Ben, I know thou hast good ideas, but by thy arrogant attitude thou wilt not make friends nor influence thine enemies." Franklin, being the wise person he was, realized that if he were to become a statesman, he needed to change. Further, he realized that in addition to his attitude of superiority, several other things about himself could stand revision, so he made a list of all of them (there were nine if my version of the story is correct).

He knew, of course, that changing everything at once was

not possible, so he set about changing these nine things one at a time over the course of nine weeks. During each week he would concentrate on just one of the items on his list. On the tenth week he would once again focus on the first trait he wanted to develop. Before long this early patriot and inventor was making many friends and influencing many people.

You, too, can make changes in your life one at a time.

Exploring What Drives Your Desire to Change

One more word about your call to action. Americans love to push themselves to "be the best they can be." I use that phrase myself in several websites I've created. However, I believe it is important to notice the direction from which your impetus for change arises. Perhaps advertising has convinced you that you aren't okay without more "things." In that case, rather than trying to make yourself feel better by finding a job that allows you to work more to get more, you would do well to explore why you value yourself so little and things so much. The same is true if your determination to get a promotion is because you believe the worth of someone is based on the prestige of his or her position.

If your drive to improve yourself comes from believing you aren't good enough right now, that you don't deserve to be loved just as you are right now, then perhaps it is time for you to realize something that took me many years to understand: Just as a seed growing into a bud and then becoming a flower is perfect at each stage of its development, so too are each of us.

For a long time I resisted this idea. As a perfectionist, I saw so many ways I wanted to improve. I thought that if I "accepted" myself just where I was, that meant I had to be "satisfied" with where I was. Now I realize that you can be dissatisfied with your life. That's okay. It's part of the impetus to change. The point is that you can both accept yourself with all your love and still set your sight on becoming someone different tomorrow. That's how I finally became the recovering perfectionist I am today. Still motivated to change. But now more comfortable with who I am.

If you know the voice encouraging you to change is your true self, then you're probably on the right track.

. . . . .

What Goal Can Change My Life?

If you've ever heard an expert speak on goal setting, you have probably heard the S.M.A.R.T. acronym. This stands for a goal that is Specific, Measurable, Action-oriented, Realistic, and Time and resource constrained. In other words, once you know, approximately, how you want your life to be different, don't be vague about it or you may not end up where you want to go.

> **ASK YOURSELF ABOUT THE END OF YOUR JOURNEY OF CHANGE**
>
> Will I be truly excited when I accomplish this goal, or will I be relieved that my work is finally over?

Unfortunately, you may resist setting goals if your prior experiences have been difficult or unsuccessful. That's why it's good to keep in mind an observation that Lea Brandenburg, an outstanding personal life coach, has made about the difference between the creation of a goal and a task. If you don't experience a resounding "yes" when creating a goal, or if you know you'll feel "relieved" when it's done, then you've just added another task to a to-do list. You haven't created a goal to which you will willingly give your energy.

However, by the time you're through answering all the questions in this book, I hope you will be able to give a resounding "yes" to your goal. In the meantime, I suggest you don't worry about whether the goal you choose will cause you to immediately and enthusiastically want to tackle it, whether it will sound like one more addition to your "to-do list," or whether it will contain the details of what you will do once you get through the gate to change. (As I discuss in CHAPTER SEVEN, one of the surest ways to prevent yourself from moving forward with a goal is to believe you have to have every single step identified and laid out in a neat line.)

As you read the rest of the questions in this chapter, you will understand why answering them will help you clarify whether the goal you think you want to reach is something you are ready to pursue.

Always remember, if you discover later that this goal isn't right for you at this time, you can always come back to this stage in the process of change. You can always rework the goal until you are sure it's the one you want to use in getting through the gate that leads beyond your comfort zone.

For now you might state your goal as a very basic target, such as "Start my own business," "Lose 10 pounds," "Call my mother more often," "Stop drinking," "Build a darkroom," "Learn French," "Go to graduate school."

Later you can add the details of where, when, and how. Questions that analyze the "why" of your goal will come later.

How Goals Evolve

Let me use a specific example to illustrate how dreams may need to be modified before you can decide whether you actually want to work toward your goal as you have stated it.

> *Peter was a workaholic with a domineering personality when his comfort zone lost its comfort.*

64

The genesis of his changed life began more than a year earlier when his wife, Ellen, increasingly complained of tension headaches and her doctor suggested she see a therapist to explore the cause. In the process of therapy, she found the courage to explore an old family myth that said women have to take whatever they get from men because "that's the way it's always been." Learning to listen to her true self and to value her own needs, she asked Peter to work less and to take a vacation now and then.

He reminded her that working more than 60 hours a week, and remaining attached to his Blackberry when he wasn't in the office, allowed her to buy the things she liked and to send their teenage children to private school. When she insisted their sons needed to see their father more than a few short hours on Sunday, he said he'd "cut down" on the hours at work. To him that meant he'd work ten instead of twelve hours a day and "try" to be available on the weekend.

But in any competition between family and Blackberry, the pull of technology (and what it signified to Peter's ego as a top salesman) always won. Eventually Ellen gave Peter an ultimatum: Work less than 50 hours a week or she would leave him.

This was Peter's call to action, his call to adventure.

Now he was finally pushed out of his comfort zone where minor adjustments in his work schedule could no long maintain the status quo. If he was to respond to this call to action, he would have to do something significantly different in his life, even though he was afraid of what less time at the office would mean to his career. He realized he had a problem on his hands and asked himself the question, "What is my goal for solving this problem?"

At first he thought a good goal would be "to improve relationships with my family," but that seemed a bit ambiguous. Wondering what might be more specific, he concluded, in a pattern that was typical of the way he made decisions, that one big trip could make up for all the unused vacations he'd built up over the years. And having heard that it helps to write down your goals, he wrote, "My goal is to travel with my family next year for one month." This seemed to him to be a clear declaration of his intent to save his marriage.

Then, after having written out his statement, but before he decided where he wanted to go, he happened to watch a show on TV about Peru. It reminded him that Machu Picchu had always seemed a mysterious and attractive destination, one his children would enjoy. He'd also been impressed with the Andes' world-class mountains and thought his children might like to climb one of them. So he then changed his goal to be even more clearly defined: "to travel to Peru for a month next year, climb a peak in the Andes, visit Machu Picchu, and learn how the indigenous highlanders maintain their traditional way of life."

Peter was sure his family would enjoy the trip he'd planned, although he knew it would be a challenge for all of them. Nevertheless, he was convinced it was a good start in doing something with the family—and in saving his marriage.

We'll use the example of Peter several more times to demonstrate how working toward a goal can proceed gradually by asking yourself questions, because you'll need those answers for unexpected twists and turns in the road ahead.

In the introduction, I said that you didn't have to write your answers to the questions in this book. However, this is one of the times when writing out your answer will make it handy for reference when you consider other questions. Keep your written goal someplace where you can be sure to find it when we do an exercise in CHAPTER SIX.

. . . . .

Would I Choose This Goal if My True Self Were in Charge and Not My Ego?

In 1994, my friend Patricia changed her career after what she thought, at the time, was a sound decision-making process over a period of months. She had been working successfully as a mammography technologist before deciding she wanted to acquire the technical skills needed by a radiation therapist. Unlike mammography, or x-rays of the breast, radiation therapy involves extreme doses of radiation administered to cancer patients to kill their body's cancer cells and requires the technician to be highly qualified.

Patricia was intrigued by the idea of helping to cure cancers and made an application for training at the renowned City of Hope Radiation Therapy Program in Duarte, California. Before then she volunteered at an outpatient radiation therapy clinic for three months to see what tasks were involved in performing the job. Then she interviewed with five medical professionals at City of Hope and, after a lengthy interview and evaluation process, she was selected to be one of eight students from a field of two-hundred applicants. Flattered that the interviewers saw her as a skilled professional with the ability to learn highly-technical skills, she was certain she would do well.

She was also proud she could tell her mother that she was "on course" to make a starting salary of $80,000 a year, which would almost double her current salary! In addition to this, she was convinced that she was making the right move when her friends enthusiastically told her she was "perfect" for that kind of work. So of course she was sure that her career was going to make her happy. It didn't. Let's examine why.

In looking back at this period of her life, Patricia can see that her decision-making process was fundamentally flawed because she listened to her ego's desire for greater salary and praise. She didn't listen to the voice in her heart that wanted to help save lives. This led to a decision based on the opinions others had of her and of her wish to please her mother. Her ego thought she would be happy. She wasn't.

What she really wanted, deep in her heart, was to be of service to the world by saving lives. True, Patricia had all the technical expertise required to be successful. Unfortunately, each day she worked as a Radiation Therapist felt like a chore she had to get through, not the uplifting experience she thought it would be. She would leave work feeling an emptiness in her life, certain she had wasted her time in the training program, and wanting to go back to doing mammograms.

Her expectation that the radiation therapy job would give her the opportunity to help save many lives was not what actually happened in her work. After only three months working in a local hospital with severely ill children and adults did she see the truth. You see, while volunteering at the outpatient facility earlier, she only came into contact with early-stage cancer patients, while the ones she was treating in the hospital were much farther advanced. Ultimately, the most Patricia's treatment could do for these gravely ill people was to reduce their pain.

Curing their cancer was almost never possible, yet saving lives had been the intention of Patricia's true self. Consequently, she left Radiation Therapy to return to mammography. She realized that in her original field of work it was critical that she take quality images so the Radiologist could make a prompt and clear diagnosis. Producing a great mammogram *did* help save lives.

Thus it was that by remaining the field of mammography that Patricia fulfilled her true heart's desire, though she cut her salary by half and faced the disappointment of friends and family. Ultimately, after brutally confronting her ego, she came to terms with the fact that money, prestige, and even her mother's approval did not make her happy.

Looking back on this experience, Patricia says she's learned that a clearly defined, specific and realistic goal based on careful decision-making with one's inner-most self is crucial to goal fulfillment. "Helping others" and "saving lives" take many forms and mean different things to different people. Interviewing well, looking the part, and being able to brag to friends and family about a job were factors that came from the encouragement of Patricia's ego, not her true self. Understanding this took courage and many first-order changes. In the end, it was worth the effort.

Today she trusts her true self more and tries to be conscious of when her ego is attempting to dictate the path she should take. Now she understands that when it comes to a career, as well as other areas of life, one's own opinion and self-respect are more important than the praise of others.

It can require great courage to counter the demands of the ego, especially when the ego believes we can't survive if we don't express an identity the ego has defined as "who we are." Encouraging the ego to support the choices of our true selves requires a dynamic that Patricia describes today as a "tight-rope walk," one that takes subtle balance and challenges her every day.

Her story illustrates an observation I've noticed for many years, especially since I've become more aware of my own true self. I've noticed that when we listen to, and then follow, the dictates of our true selves, we become a source of kindness and healing in the world more easily than we would if our ego led us to act so that we would be praised for our good deeds. Or as Albert Schweitzer observed, "I don't know what your destiny will be, but one thing I know: the only ones among you who will be really happy are those who will have sought and found how to serve." When that service comes from deep within you, it is a joy to do whatever you choose to do.

When you make choices from your highest self, you will not only try to meet your own needs, you will take into consideration the needs of others. You can see this at work in Rotary International, a service organization whose motto is "To serve unselfishly." In order to know whether the words and actions of members are true to that motto, they are encouraged to ask themselves whether what they are planning to do or say (1) is true, (2) is fair to everybody, (3) will lead to goodwill and better friendship, and (4) will be useful to everybody. Why not imagine you are an honorary Rotarian and recognize that everything you do impacts others?

> **ASK YOURSELF ABOUT EGO**
>
> When I look back over my life and remember the times that I felt most happy and contented, were my actions generally driven by my ego or was I led by my true self?

. . . . .

What Are the Advantages and Disadvantages of Reaching My Goal?

In deciding whether you want to reach the goal you've set for yourself, you first need to realize what will probably happen if you *don't* make a change in your life.

When you evaluate your plans from this perspective, it wouldn't be surprising if you discovered not changing jobs will leave you in a boring, restrictive job. Not working toward saving money for a trip to Europe will mean you won't see parts of the world you've long wanted to explore. Not resolving an ongoing family feud will mean you'll continue to fight with your brother. And it is clear that Peter, in the previous story, clearly sees that not cutting back on his hours and not spending more time with the family means he may be headed for divorce. If he does what his wife wants, he will avoid a divorce, which is certainly to his advantage.

Unfortunately, what keeps anyone stuck in old ruts is that *there are advantages in not changing.* The advantage of not accomplishing your goal can mean you will save money (by not having to pay for classes). You will not have to learn a new skill (which might be difficult and time-consuming). You will not have to move or change jobs (ditto). You will not have to go through the discomfort of losing weight (double ditto). In other words, you will not have to spend the time and energy it would take to do any of the things that accomplishing your goal would require.

However, just as staying where you are has both advantages and disadvantages, stepping into the unknown offers both the possibility of success and the potential of dangers and unexpected obstacles you may not want to face. But if facing danger holds you back, consider the consequence of avoiding risk, of drawing around you a curtain of "safety" and "security." Right now, it may feel comforting, eventually it can feel claustrophobic.

If you are hesitant to set out on the road to adventure, you may want to avoid the potential burdens of trying to reach a goal that in the end may not be possible. But if you *don't* answer the call to adventure and action, some day in the future you may discover that you're left with a sense of disappointment in yourself for not having had the courage to risk the unknown. True, you will have avoided some trials and tribulations, but you will also have missed the chance for what could be an exhilarating adventure.

What happens if you risk of going through the gate and *aren't* able to reach your dreams? Well, then you will have tried. That, in itself, can provide great satisfaction. Besides, what you learn in failure will be worth far more in considering any future goals you want to pursue than you'll gain from sitting at home behind your comfort curtain.

Weighing the Benefits and Burdens of Change

Exploring the advantages of staying where you are or moving forward can be difficult because the choices are not always simple. Sometimes it can feel as though you are falling off a cliff into the unknown when you decide to take one path rather than another.

Once again I'll use Patricia to demonstrate that the process of making a decision is seldom smooth. This time she had to make a decision when she was offered the chance to change from her current mammography job (A) to a potential mammography job (B). It was not a position she sought, but it was offered to her because she'd previously worked for that hospital part-time and they liked her work.

In order to evaluate whether a change in jobs was what she really wanted, we began by listing the basic factors in her current and potential positions. Here are her options as we outlined them:

JOB A: CURRENT JOB	JOB B: POTENTIAL JOB
1. 40 minutes from home	15 minutes from home
2. No increase in salary	$10,000/per year increase in salary
3. Work 4 days a week, including some evenings and weekends	Work 5 days a week, free on weekends and holidays
4. Respect of co-workers	Unknown

That's quite a mix of factors, not unlike a situation with which you may be struggling. So how did she weigh the advantages and disadvantages of each job to see how a job change would most likely work out? To begin with, we used a common approach in evaluating which choice would, over-all, be preferable by following a formula that uses a rating scale.

And if the words "formula" and "rating scale" cause your brain to freeze, hang in there, because learning how to do this can be helpful in many situations. So, using a rating scale of "1" to "10," which we used earlier when choosing a goal, with "1" being not important and "10" being very important, she looked at each of the factors in changing jobs.

1. Drive time was a "10" in favor of Job B, while Job A got a "4". It wasn't that driving was absolutely horrible, it just isn't fun to spend time on the freeways.

2. She thought of all the things the extra money could buy and the travel she could do, so the money offered by Job B was given a "7". She gave a "6" for the salary from Job A. It wasn't bad, just not as good as Job B.

3. Evenings and weekends free was a "9" in favor of Job B. However, realizing her partner could continue to take care of himself when she wasn't home, she gave her current job a "5".

4. This factor was very difficult to quantify, for it involved respect and arose from the fact that it was not Patricia's style to get involved in office politics or to share personal information with her co-workers. Consequently, she has sometimes been seen as aloof and has had a hard time being accepted in several places where she worked. But she'd worked for several years at Job A and the people there appreciated her skills, held her in high regard, and sought her opinion about work-related problems. This was something that was very satisfying when compared with other jobs she'd had where co-workers thought she was "stuck-up." There was no guarantee that she would be treated the same respectful way in Job B. Thus she decided that having respect from co-workers was a "10" in favor of Job A. She gave Job B a "1", since the factor of respect could go either way there.

Adding her scores together, there was a "27" in favor of switching jobs and a "25" in favor of staying. That clearly wasn't enough to decide one way or another. Therefore, to help her explore her options further, I used a technique with her that I've used with many of my clients. In doing the exercise she was able to make a clear and satisfying decision. I'll tell you about her choice in CHAPTER SIX, after you explore some questions that need to be answered before you're ready to do the exercise yourself.

· · · · ·

What is the Primary Motivation for Wanting to Reach My Goal?

The *advantages* of achieving your goal are not the same as the *motivation* for accomplishing your goal. For example, wanting to clean the garage will result in a clean garage. That is a clear advantage. If you want to mobilize the energy you will need to do all that work, however, it is best if you ask yourself "why" you want a clean garage, which is probably because you're tired of spending much too long in searching for something you need among all the "stuff" in boxes stacked precariously on top of one another. So the *motivation* of "creating an efficient system for finding things," while close to the *advantage* of achieving your goal, will hopefully be strong enough to get you out of bed on Saturday and start pulling boxes out of the garage and onto the driveway for a long sorting job.

> ### ASK YOURSELF ABOUT MOTIVATION
>
> Out of all the reasons why I shouldn't pursue my goal at this time, what makes the most sense? Why?
>
> When looking at the reasons why I should work toward my goal, what is the most important? Why?

If we look for a moment at the goal Peter had of wanting to visit Peru, we can see that the advantage of going there is that he would be doing something enjoyable, he'd get away from work at the office, he'd see a different part of the world, and he would have a chance to rebuild his relationship with his family.

However, on the paper where he'd written his goal he added his motivation that, "I want to do something that will please my wife so she won't want to get a divorce." Keeping that motivation in mind was more important to him than simply the pleasure of finally going on a vacation.

When you decide the primary motivation for changing your life, i.e., for reaching your goal, be sure to write it down. Then keep that piece of paper with the one on which you wrote your goal. Soon you'll be adding another piece of paper to those two—and then you'll use them all in the crucial step of getting through the gate to change.

· · · · ·

What Will My Life Look Like When I Reach My Goal?

With all the demands we have on our time and energy, it's not surprising that many goals fall by the wayside. One of the reasons this happens is because we often don't have clear reminders of our goal where we can see them the way dirty clothes remind us to do the washing and an empty refrigerator tells us it's time for grocery shopping.

Let's think about the brain again. The brain doesn't develop new neurons or create new pathways if we simply say, "Brain, build more neurons." That's because we use the language of images to communicate with our brains. A more svelte body. A diploma. A new car. Setting out on an exciting cruise. A sleeping baby. Being held and loved by someone special. The smile on the face of a friend. Each of these positive images holds within it the energy that represents what a change in belief and behavior will accomplish.

However, we also speak with our brains through negative images. The scowling face of a parent. Floundering in the water when you were a child and fell into a pool. The screeching of brakes and a car crashing into yours. Standing in front of the class and forgetting the lines for the school play.

We can allow images of fear and embarrassment to reinforce old beliefs and keep old neurons firing in old patterns. On the other hand, we can create new images based on the belief that life can be different and thus build new pathways that allow us to act in new ways and have new consequences.

That is why in working with people for many years that I encourage them to use imagery to discover what they imagine their life will look like when they reach their goal. Then, I help them create a symbol or picture based on their image of the future that can give them the energy they will need if they are to be successful in making their dream a reality.

Of course, if their picture is to help them accomplish their goal, it needs to be strong and an accurate representation of their motivation for change. Here are some examples:

> *Marco works for an authoritarian boss who allows no deviation from company rules, although the business could more effectively operate with greater flexibility. Now Marco is considering opening a competing business, using as his main motivation the ability to set his own schedule. He says a picture of a sailboat would help because it will remind him that he can take time off during the week to sail with his friends.*

> *Eleanor loves historical novels but has never been to Europe, where many of the stories are set. Her motivation is the opportunity to experience places she's fallen in love with through hundreds of books. Because of her modest salary, however, it will require major belt-tightening and packed lunches. Nevertheless, for her a picture of money*

will not be as powerful as a picture of the guards at Buckingham Palace.

Marshall loves his children. He also loves beer, wine and whatever else he can get his hands on. A high-functioning alcoholic, for years he's been able to hide much of his drinking from family and friends. Recently, however, he almost had an accident when one of his children was in the car and this frightened him enough that he's decided to go to AA. That will only be the first step, however, and he knows he needs reinforcement to continue attending. So he takes a picture of his three children and on the bottom of it writes "For them." This is, for him, a powerful reminder that he wants to be around for them and is determined not to let his drinking harm them in any way. As time goes on, he may come to realize that not drinking is something he needs to do for himself as well, but if this picture gets him started on the road to sobriety, it's a good start.

Marjorie wants to stop having pointless arguments with her sister. At first, she thought a trophy could be a good image; she would surely deserve a trophy if she could remain calm and serene whenever her sister attempts to goad her into an argument. But as she thinks more about it, she realizes that what she wants is not only to stop feeling she has to be right, but to rekindle the relationship she had with her sister when they were young. For her, an old photo of the two of them sitting on a swing together did the trick.

Now it's time for you to draw a picture or symbol to remind you of your goal, keeping in mind that you won't be graded on your artistic talent. There are many options. You might want to cut out a picture of your goal from a catalog, newspaper, or magazine and paste it onto a piece of paper in a color you particularly like. A collage of small objects, bits of newspaper, cloth, and anything that suits your fancy can, taken as a whole, represent your goal. Imagine what you can do with digital cameras, Photoshop, and pictures downloaded from the internet. I am certain that you will be able to create a picture of your future that will be a strong reminder of your goal, an image your brain can use to start the creation of new neuronal pathways leading to success.

Peter started on his journey to change by using the motivation to keep his family together through his trip to Peru. So he created a collage of the lost city of Machu Picchu, together with a picture of the Andes and other places in Peru (cutting them from travel brochures), and assembled them with a picture of him and his family in the center.

Keep your picture with the statement of your goal and the statement of your primary motivation for reaching your goal. Soon you'll have a chance to put all these pieces together and get through the gate that stands between the Land of Wish-and-Want, where you have been operating up to this point, and the Land of Will-Do, where accomplishment lies.

If you want your life to change, reflect on these questions from CHAPTER FOUR:

- *How do I want my life to be different?*

- *What is my call to action?*

- *What goal can change my life?*

- *Would I choose this goal if my true self were in charge and not my ego?*

- *What are the advantages and disadvantages of reaching my goal?*

- *What is the primary motivation for wanting to reach my goal?*

- *What will my life look like when I reach my goal?*

CHAPTER FIVE

What Beliefs Might Sabotage My Goals?

I t is easy to get tripped on the path to change by stumbling blocks placed there by circumstances over which we have no control. Unfortunately, too often we sabotage ourselves by adding our own obstacles created from unexplored patterns of the old belief-action-consequences-belief cycle.

Add that resistance to the ego's insistence that past dictates the future — that what you've stuffed into your "backpack" can't be taken out without destroying your identity—and you are unlikely to make it through the gate to change, let alone move on from there to success.

Let me give you a couple of examples.

The first is the story of a woman in her mid-sixties whom I'll call Margaret. Her son committed suicide thirty years ago. Even after all these years and lots of therapy she has focused on his death as the reason for not being able to experience joy and pleasure in life. Her ego gets very defensive whenever it's suggested that she let her son go and move on. "How can I?" she cries, pulling out the guilt card, insisting that she "should" have prevented his death, and doing everything else she can to avoid giving up her depression.

She complains that she wants to feel happy, and has even gone to several therapists for help, but none of them can help her. When they begin to dig deeper, they discover a major belief that if she got "well" (that is, if her depression went away), her husband would leave her. That sounds strange, but it turns out that her husband's part in the drama of her life comes from his belief, based on his childhood experience, that he was put on this earth to take care of others. He needs his wife to *need* him as much as she needs her husband to take care of *her*. If she's well, she won't need him, he won't feel needed, and he'll have to find someone else who needs a rescuer.

It's exactly this kind of circular reasoning that keeps us stuck on this side of the gate to change.

Incidentally, when a new client tells a therapist, "I'm sure you can help me. None of the ten therapists I've seen so far were able to understand me," it can be ego-boosting to a new therapist. She or he thinks, "I'll be the one who helps this poor woman create a better life for herself." A more experienced therapist will know that the chance is one-thousand-to-one that the client's ego is holding onto some defense that is sure to sabotage any real work the client claims she wants to do.

Another example of the way we can delude ourselves can be seen in the case of an alcoholic who began drinking and using marijuana when he was fifteen. While he may have begun out of curiosity, he soon found drinking an easy solution to the angst of adolescence. He wanted to fit in, to be the life of the party. That only seemed to happen when he was drinking with his buddies. As the years slipped by and he continued to use alcohol as a social crutch, he convinced himself that alcohol was the only ingredient that enabled him to function.

When he was thirty, he had his eyes on a woman who said she wouldn't marry an alcoholic. He was sure she was the one for him and claimed he wasn't an alcoholic, believing he could stop drinking any time he wanted. In fact, he did stop, for awhile. However, he then discovered his social skills without a glass in his hand were those of a fifteen-year-old, not the sophistication of the thirty-year-olds around him.

"I'm not an alcoholic," he continued to tell himself. "Just because alcohol and a hit of pot help me function doesn't mean I'm addicted." So he reached for a beer, or two or three and, feeling relaxed, stepped into a party where he found a new woman, one who didn't care whether or not he drank, and who perhaps needed a companion to support her own addictive behavior.

Thus his belief that he has to drink causes him to use drink as a social lubricant, which makes him feel better. Must be the alcohol, he concludes. He conveniently skips over the fact that other aspects of his life may be falling apart because of alcohol. But his need for social acceptance is so great that his ego clings to alcohol as the way to function around others. If he were to get in touch with his true self and listen to the voice of love and self-care inside of him, he might discover that he could develop another belief, one in which he found value within himself and in connection to something beyond his limited ego.

There is a paradox here, however, as there often is for alcoholics. That is because it has long been recognized that an alcoholic seldom takes steps to stop drinking until he's sick and tired of being sick and tired of all the problems alcohol has caused in his life. In fact, if he goes to a therapist who works to build up his "self-esteem" (on the theory that he will then have the courage to join AA or enter into a treatment program), his new-found self-esteem can be counterproductive. Why? Because having an expert tell him he's "okay" is not as effective as having someone he respects remind him of the mess he's made of his life. Self-prescribed alcohol and drugs are great anesthetics that cover pain and disappointment in oneself.

With this kind of reasoning, it is not surprising that many alcoholics never change and never recover.

. . . . .

Am I Willing to Move Beyond Resistance by Honestly Examining My Beliefs?

One of the problems with beliefs that create resistance is that we are usually blind to their effect. That is especially true with goals we've tried to reach before but never seem to accomplish because we stop ourselves, or let circumstances stop us. However, if you are really serious about getting through the gate to change, dig deeply into your backpack and make a list of all the obstacles, problems, and challenges you are most likely to face along the path to success. Notice those that concern you most and the beliefs you have that are related to those potential stumbling blocks. This will make it much easier to finalize your goal and prepare to step into the Land of Will-Do.

Courage to examine beliefs with an open mind is an important step in understanding how beliefs can sabotage goals. Understanding how those beliefs arose allows you to do something about them. For example, if you realize you are a perfectionist, you can take steps to counter that tendency by doing the simple exercises on the next page.

TAKE ACTION

Counter Perfectionism With Acceptance

[Are you a perfectionist? Take the perfectionist test in the AP-PENDIX.]

1. *When you begin the day, hold your arms out wide, point them up to the sky, and say, "Whatever." The term "whatever" indicates your willingness to accept whatever the day will bring without trying to force it into the shape you want to make it, which may cause the day to be more difficult than it needs to be. At the end of the day, hold your arms out, point them down and say, "So what." Use the "so what" as an indication that you are willing to release whatever didn't go precisely as you would have liked.*

2. *There is another variation of accepting each day just as it is: Fill a small bowl or pitcher at the beginning of the day with water. At the end of the day, pour the water out, perhaps using it to water a plant. Use this routine to acknowledge that each day is sufficient for itself and that you consciously release all the expectations you may have had that the day should have contained more than it was able to provide.*

3. *Every morning say to yourself, "Until now I've not known how to be anything but a perfectionist. Now I'm learning to accept myself and life on more comfortable and easy terms. I will do whatever I can comfortably do, but I will not insist I have to exceed reasonable standards for success."*

Have I Allowed Regrets and Grudges to Keep Me Stuck in the Past?

If you look deeply into your backpack, you'll likely find some all-too-human baggage that keeps many of us from moving forward. These are the multiple grudges and resentments we hold against others, to say nothing of the regrets we have about our own behaviors in the past.

Fortunately, there is a way to get past regrets and open your mind to possibilities for success in the future. Begin by asking yourself questions about the situation that has you stuck in the past.

1. What am I holding onto that keeps me focused on the past?

2. What part did I play, even though unintentionally, in the loss of an expectation that things would have turned out differently?

3. Am I willing to forgive myself and/or others in order to release guilt and energy that has kept me trapped in the past?

4. What did I learn from whatever it is I regret?

5. Why do I want to release the regret I've now chosen to let go of?

Once you have answered those questions as well as you can, think of a picture that represents your regret and draw it on a piece of paper, or just hold the picture in your imagination. Then plan a ceremony in which you will get rid of the paper (again, either in reality or in your imagination) by a method that can actually get rid of it, such as dropping it into a shredder and watching it become a zillion unusable pieces. Perhaps you could flush it down the toilet or burn it.

Before getting rid of the paper in the ceremony of release, acknowledge your readiness to let go by saying, "I am ready to release my regret that . . ." and then complete the sentence. For example, you might say, "I am ready to release my regret that I didn't treat my friend more kindly."

Before releasing the paper, add a simple good-bye statement, such as, "Good-bye regret" . . . "Good-bye dream" . . . "Good-bye expectation." Then, as you release the paper and watch it disappear, taking the image of your regret with it, let yourself fully experience the inner peace and calm that comes from giving up regrets and accepting life exactly as it has turned out to be.

Another aspect of getting past regrets is the need to forgive yourself and/or others. Of course, sometimes we simply fail to forgive because we don't know how, so on the next page you can learn to forgive what you (and others) can no longer do anything about, which will free up energy to use on working toward your goal.

ASK YOURSELF ABOUT REGRETS

Do I often find myself focused on what "was" or "could have been" if only I hadn't been so weak, so unwise, so unlucky?

Do I often think of what might have been if only such-and-such hadn't happened, or if only someone else had done what he or she was supposed to do?

Is it possible that my view of what could be in my future is blocked by images of defeat and failure of the past?

What picture, image, symbol, or statement best represents a regret that is holding me back?

How will I get rid of that picture, image, symbol, or statement?

When I teach people how to forgive, I always begin by reminding them that no one wakes up in the morning with the intention to screw up his or her life. True, some people *seem* to want to mess up the lives of

TAKE ACTION

A Powerful Forgiveness Exercise

Imagine that a person (including yourself) who has offended you in some way is standing in front of you as he or she was at the time that person said or did something hurtful. Keeping that image in your mind, say:

> *"When you said or did_____ ,I was hurt and angry. I would have preferred you _____ . But you did not. When I think about what you said or did, I have let myself feel anger, resentment, pain, bitterness. I have held onto my demand that you should have said or done some-thing different. I no longer choose to hold onto the tension and hurt that accom-panies my memory of what you said or did."*

> *"Therefore, I cancel the demands, expectations, and conditions I placed on you that you should have _____ . You are totally responsible for your own actions and deeds."*

> *"I now send my love [or, if that word is too strong, acceptance] to you as a human being, just as you were and are now."*

Then imagine that your love or acceptance is going out to the other person. Take your time to experience how your body feels when you release the conditions you placed on this person to be someone he or she (and that includes you) did not know how to be or, for whatever reason, was unable to be.

others, but that's only because they have a distorted belief that making someone else's life miserable will make theirs happier. In the end, it doesn't work, but at the moment it may appear to them to be the only way to get their needs met.

In any case, I believe that we each do the best we can with what we know that day. If we pay attention, we learn new things every day so the next day there is less chance we'll make the same mistakes. It is from that perspective that I use the simple forgiveness exercise on the preceding page that you may want to use if resentment or hurt feelings are keeping you from moving forward.

Always remember this: if you have a hard time forgiving yourself because you believe you "should have" known something earlier in your life that you are just now learning, you are setting up stumbling blocks you can do without. Therefore, if you wish you'd have been smarter sooner, I would like to give you a statement that has been extremely helpful for many people. It goes like this:

> *Until now I haven't known how to . . . [WHATEVER IT IS THAT YOU DON'T KNOW HOW TO DO]," but now I am learning how to . . .[WHATEVER IT IS YOU HAVEN'T KNOWN HOW TO DO AND ARE WILLING TO LEARN].*

That is a true statement and one that includes the hopeful message that it is never too late to learn lessons in life.

There is one more matter you should explore before approaching the gate to change. This is your belief about a person who can come between you and your goal. One of the reasons it is hard to break away from family myths and the rules and rituals that supported family beliefs is because it can seem disloyal to walk another path, to believe something your family doesn't believe, to do something of which your family won't approve.

Consider the important people in your life and notice what you think they will say when they hear your goal, when they know you're working toward it, and when you reach it. You see, one of the major barriers to success can be the power we hand to others who would be "disturbed" if we achieved our goal. We need to take their views into consideration, of course. But if one of the internal barriers is the fear that others won't be able to handle the change we want to make in our lives, we are wise to notice whether their potential disappointment gives us an excuse for not going forward because we're really afraid we'll disappoint ourselves.

Sometimes past regrets and grudges become heavy burdens in our backpacks, or we push them in carts along the path to what we hope will be a changed life. We seem to be unable to drop them in order to move forward. Often, it's hard to recognize when we've let this happen, so be sure to look very carefully for insidious beliefs that others won't be able to handle your success, or that you "can't" do something because someone else didn't do what they were supposed to do. If you don't handle these issues now, before deciding you're willing to do whatever it takes to reach your goal once you get through the gate to change, I can almost guarantee you that you'll meet these issues on the other side.

. . . . .

Do I Need to Allow More Love to Flow Into My Life?

Love, they say, makes the world go 'round. Love helps us tolerate those who are intolerant toward us. Love allows us to widen our appreciation for the other person. Love supports our true self and the path it asks us to walk.

However, we can sometimes prevent ourselves from receiving (and giving) the love that is essential for living life fully and smoothing out many bumps on the road to success. Therefore, I would like to encourage you to increase love in your life by giving you an exercise inspired by one I experienced in a workshop on creativity with John O'Donohue, gifted Irish poet and former priest, for it demonstrates the force that love can play in all our lives.

In order to have this story make a difference in your life — so that you can make a difference in the lives of others — I suggest you read this as though it *could* actually happen to you.

> *Imagine one day you are feeling very stressed out and burdened by conflicts at work and arguments at home. With your career uncertain and your relationship rocky, you decide to drive to your favorite spot overlooking the ocean. In the past this has helped center you and today you hope it will do the trick.*
>
> *Then as you sit on a rock and stare far into the horizon, your attention is drawn to a boat. It seems to be like every other boat on the water, but you sense that there is something special about it and can't stop watching it as it slowly approaches land.*
>
> *Then, you notice several people in the boat and they are looking at you as though they are very pleased you are there, as though you are exactly the person they have come to see. When they pull the boat up onto the beach, they don't say anything. They only walk toward you and smile. But ah, the smile and the look in their eyes conveys a gentle love you've never felt before. The kindness that is streaming from them into your very soul is so full of compassion that it melts all that has grown wounded and hard within you.*
>
> *No one has ever looked at you like this before. You feel no need to be ashamed or to pretend or to avoid*

them. No need to flee. In the presence of their gaze upon you, you realize they are allowing you to be absolutely yourself. In that look there is no judgment, or need to feel guilty. There is no burden or expectation, only the simple beauty of love.

As you allow yourself to feel the infinite tenderness of that loving gaze looking directly into your soul, you know they know all about you and about the conflicts and confusion you carry within your heart. They know who you are and are proud of who you are despite what you see as your imperfections. And so, as you continue to feel their gaze upon you, your intense need to be right—and to win the arguments you've been determined to win—falls away as you are filled with their acceptance of who you are just as you are.

It is then that you close your eyes, wanting to bring inside the deepest part of you the full gift of their love. As you do so, you promise yourself that from now on you will try to look at yourself, and accept yourself, with the same tenderness, recognition, compassion and love.

You are not sure how long your eyes have been closed, but when you open them, the people and the boat are no longer there. You spend a few moments wondering where they came from and where they have gone. Are they emissaries of a higher being? Did you just imagine this experience? Soon, however, you know in the deepest part of your soul that this really happened. You didn't imagine it. And you realize that the love they offer is the foundation of all life.

As you get in your car to return home, you carry with you that gaze of love and acceptance. When you see your family, when you go to work, when you walk down the street, you know that some-

thing profound has shifted within you, for when you look at others, you see them with the same tenderness and compassion you felt from the visitors on the beach. And each person looks back at you with a look of genuine joy in being accepted just as they are.

This simple shift in your awareness does not make all your problems go away, but they now seem so much easier to accept. And in that acceptance comes the belief that you are not victim of what someone else thinks of you. Now you can recognize the part you play in issues that have, previously, seemed to be out of your control. And one thing is certain, love will play a larger role in your life in the future.

If this story opened your heart, if in your imagination you could understand that a look of unconditional love can be healing, it is important to know that you have that kind of love within you right now. Otherwise, you wouldn't have been able to "imagine" it happening!

Therefore, if this exercise has opened your heart, consider what might happen if you chose to look at others not with judgment, but with love, great gentleness and compassion? We don't know all the things that have gone into making others who they are today. Yet they are who they are, whether or not we think they *should* be that way. They are who they are, even though they may be happier if they were able to change some part of themselves that causes them distress. But I can tell you this: I have learned over many years that if we can accept all of who *we* are, including our shadow side, we are less frightened by the shadow side of *others*.

Until we learn to look upon others with love and acceptance, how can we expect others to look upon us with love? We all have a radar that can pick up the signal someone is sending that says, "I don't like you. You aren't my kind of person. I don't want to extend myself to bring you into my circle of friends." What might the world be like if we all loved ourselves and shared that love with everyone else? How much easier might it be to reach the goal you set for yourself when you smooth the path with love?

This brings us back to the idea I talked about in the beginning of CHAPTER TWO, when I said that we can't change unless we accept what is true about us at this moment. Similarly, when we reject other people because of who they are, we make it harder for them to open themselves to change and to being more fully themselves.

ASK YOURSELF ABOUT LOVE

Am I willing to love myself and others so that I can make my life easier and, in the process, make the world a better place for everyone?

As I write these words, I remember Abigail, a friend from more than forty years ago, who showed in many way that she accepted me without first requiring me to be different. She certainly saw my many flaws. However, the fact that she didn't demand I be someone I didn't yet know how to be meant that I was free to be myself around her. And thus her friendship was the beginning of many positive changes I was able to make as I moved through the process of change I describe in this book.

· · · · ·

Would a Therapist and/or Life Coach Be Helpful?

Since negative beliefs and resistance often operate outside our consciousness, it can be very helpful to get professional assistance if you think you want to change but never seem able to do it. Whether you're motivated by pain to change your life or by inspiration, there are people who are trained to help make the process easier. And since there are basically two categories of professional help that approach goal-setting in slightly different ways, you'll make the best progress toward changing your life if you understand the benefits they each offer.

Originally, as everyone knows, Freud got the be-a-better-person ball rolling with psychoanalysis, which generally required several years of intense therapy. In that technique the analyst reflected back to the patient (they weren't called "clients" until more than a half century later) what the patient said, so that memories and fears, as well as other things buried in one's backpack, could be exposed to the light. This worked for many people who could afford to see a psychiatrist, but it was out of range for most people because of the cost and the long time frame. And of course, it didn't work for everyone.

Gradually, new forms of therapy arose that expanded on the "why" and "how" of behaviors that arise from unconscious needs and motivations. In these therapies, the focus is on a person's inner world and can be valuable when people need help in understanding how their past is keeping them from moving forward. After all, there are many reasons we get stuck in the past. Some of those reasons have to do with family patterns, trauma, abuse, addictions, genetic disposition, temperament, and personality styles. Many people with these emotional blocks have been greatly helped by therapists trained in various schools of behavioral and insight therapy.

However, in recent years the helping profession has realized that when people are functioning fairly well they don't need to spend a lot of time exploring the past. They need to focus on the future. This is where personal development coaching, life coaching, and success coaching come in. Coaches encourage people to find the purpose for their lives, express the highest qualities of the human spirit, live with vitality, and use one's talents and skills to make a difference in the world. Increasingly, corporations pay for executive coaching to help their employees maximize their skills and move up the corporate ladder, benefiting both the employee and the company.

It is said that with a coach you can "produce fulfilling results in your personal and professional life." A coach will "provide support to enhance the skills, resources, and creativity" that you already have. A coach will "elicit solutions and strategies" to "enhance the quality of your life." All of that sounds enticing. But is that the kind of support you need?

How can you decide whether you might need a therapist or a coach, both, or neither? Let's look at it this way.

Therapy is helpful for someone who feels stuck in low gear, unable to get up the hill to where the gate is waiting, or

---

WHEN CHOOSING A THERAPIST, REMEMBER THAT . . .

There is no one-size-fits-all approach in the field of therapy, as in almost every other professional field. So don't assume that because a therapist was good for someone else that he or she will be the right therapist for you.

The more experience and training therapists have, the more likely they will charge a higher fee. Someone at the local mental health center, on the other hand, who is a therapist-in-training may charge little or nothing and may still be a good fit for you. Don't count quality only on the basis of how much someone charges.

If you aren't willing to participate fully in therapy, you'll not make the progress you want.

---

who seems to be trapped in the Land of Wish-and-Want. So if you can't seem to get beyond self-defeating beliefs that you aren't smart enough, aren't good enough, don't deserve to be successful, etc., consider seeing a therapist. He or she can help you explore those messages and help you become willing and able to do what you need to do to reach your goal and change your life. Such therapy need not require months or years of digging into your past to expose a belief that has convinced you that you aren't able to successfully make the change in life that you want to make.

Once you get rid of some of the junk in your backpack, life coaches can help you make the last little push through the gate, and can guide you when you're in the Land of Will-Do. It certainly helps to have someone encourage and prod us to be our very best. However, not everyone can afford to hire a coach. Not all coaches are as good as their advertisement would

---

WHEN CHOOSING A COACH, REMEMBER THAT . . .

There is tremendous variety in the quality and experience of those who call themselves "coaches." So be sure to explore their experience in the area you want to pursue. Also, ask if you may talk with one of their clients. Reputable coaches should be willing to put you in touch with clients they have helped. If there are testimonials on their websites, ask if they would be willing to let you get in touch with writers of those testimonials.

Coaching is not a magic wand. There is a real commitment you must make if the process is going to be successful—and worth the fairly large amount of money you'll be handing over, to say nothing of the work you'll do.

have you believe. Not everyone needs a coach. For example, if you know the steps you need to take and are already doing those things on your own, a coach may not provide enough additional information and guidance to be worth the high cost. And because a coach primarily helps you define your goals and keeps you focused on them, you may have the self discipline to do that yourself.

On the other hand, if you are the kind of person who knows what you *should* do but who has a tendency to procrastinate, you may find it valuable to have a coach who will give you a kick-in-the-pants, keep your feet to the fire, or in some other way help you change your "shoulds" into "I wills." Also, a coach may be able to show you more options than you had previously considered. That kind of encouragement may be well worth the cost.

If you want your life to change, reflect on these questions from CHAPTER FIVE:

- *What beliefs might sabotage my goals?*

- *Am I willing to move beyond resistance by honestly examining my beliefs?*

- *Have I allowed regrets and grudges to keep me stuck in the past?*

- *Do I need to allow my love to flow into my life?*

- *Would a therapist and/or life coach be helpful?*

CHAPTER SIX

How Committed Am I to Changing My Life?

Until this point in the book, you've been answering questions that are important for getting *to* the gate to change. You've looked at yourself and your strengths as honestly as you can, explored how your past has influenced your life today, spent time in seeing how you might answer your call to action with a goal that seems doable, and explored ways you might sabotage your efforts.

Now we come to such an *essential* goal-achieving question that it is the focus of an entire chapter. If you have paid careful attention to earlier questions, by the time you finish this chapter you will know whether you are ready to work toward your goal, or whether you need to go back and reword your goal statement.

In the fairy tales and adventure stories of childhood, as you are sure to remember, the hero or heroine finds many challenges in the land on the other side of the gate. That place, which I refer to as the Land of Will-Do, is described by Joseph Campbell in *The Hero With a Thousand Faces* this way:

This fateful region of both treasure and danger may be variously represented: as a distant land, a forest, a kingdom, underground, beneath the waves, or above the sky, a secret island, lofty mountaintop, or profound dream state; but it is always a place of strangely fluid and polymorphous beings, unimaginable torments, superhuman deeds, and impossible delight.

You hope that when you get through the gate you will find only the most pleasant of experiences. The chances are, however, that you may run into a few unpleasant experiences as well. Of course, you won't know what you'll find until you leave the land of familiar comfort, the Land of Wish-and-Want, which Roger expects to happen as he continues his journey.

The Heroic Journey

STAGE TWO

When we left our potential hero, Roger (whom we met in CHAPTER FOUR), was in the middle of a conversation with the guardian at a gate leading to change. As you may remember, the guard asked, "Why do you want me to unlock the gate for you? Why do you want to leave the sanctuary of home and hearth and set out into the wild unknown? Don't you realize you could be set upon by robbers? Vicious animals could attack you!"

Unless the guardian is convinced Roger is truly dedicated to his journey of learning, he will insist the young man remain in the town, for he has seen many people claim they want to leave, only to have them return before nightfall, frightened by lengthening shadows.

Yet brave Roger has an answer for the guardian of the gate: "I have to leave because I have a burning dream to learn about herbs and treatment for the sick and the injured. I won't feel whole until I go out into the world and discover what I cannot find in the limitations of this place. I am sure that somewhere on the other side of the locked gate I will find what I *must* find if I am to fulfill my destiny. Let me go and, if I am successful, I will return and tell you what I have found."

The guardian realizes Roger is a very committed young man, so he says, "I see you're determined to go through the gate, but I must tell you that I require a payment from each person who wants me to unlock the gate. What are you willing to give up? It must be something you prize."

Roger hadn't expected this and takes a few moments to decide which possession he will part with. He doesn't have much with him, only the food his mother packed and the small amount of money she put into his satchel. Then he has an idea. He will give up the familiar comfort of his home, he tells the guardian, for that is worth much. He doesn't make his offer lightly, but in his heart he is certain that when he has learned what he wants to learn that it will be worth the sacrifice.

This determination convinces the guardian that Roger should be allowed to pursue his goal. As he turns to the gate and rattles his keys, Roger's heart beats faster, imagining what lies on the other side.

What is interesting, however, is that the guard doesn't actually unlock the gate! The fact is that the gate to change is *already* unlocked. It only stands in such a way that it *appears* to be locked, for it is comforting to the townsfolk to believe that they are protected from the outside world. The truth is that anyone could leave at any time. Yet the guardian does nothing to dispute the illusion that he holds the key to whether someone can leave because it is his job to prevent people from getting injured if they are unprepared to take the risk of change.

At the same time, the guardian provides a handy excuse for those who aren't dedicated to change. "The gate is locked," they say. The paradox is that until someone is willing to challenge the guardian, he or she can't discover that the lock doesn't work.

Having shown the courage to confront the guardian, Roger walks through the gate and enters a period of trials, tribulations, and exciting possibilities in the land outside the comfort of home.

TO BE CONTINUED

Engaging the "Will"

Are you ready to get past the guardian at the gate that stands between the Land of Wish-and-Want and the Land of Will-Do? Good.

Now, to help you see just how ready you are to proceed, I've designed an exercise that has been highly successful in helping many people know whether they are ready to move toward their goals, or whether they need to reevaluate their goal and the advantages and disadvantages of changing their lives.

Before giving you that exercise, however, there is something you must do first: Decide what you will give up!

Every worthwhile change requires sacrifice. That's why so few people make the changes in life they *say* they want to make, and why now is the time to explore what you will surrender to success.

You may not need to give up much, but in the act of relinquishing something that makes you comfortable in your present circumstances, you are taking the first step in acknowledging that making progress requires effort.

> **ASK YOURSELF ABOUT SACRIFICE**
>
> What do I need to relinquish if I am going to get through the gate to change?
>
> Am I willing to give that up? Why?

Consider carefully what you will freely offer as a sacrifice for the potential of success. Once you have decided what that will be, proceed with this exercise. Giving up something will allow you to have a lighter step and more resolve to change your life

Once you are sure that you will set aside a comfort of the past, here is what you do.

1. First, take out the paper on which you wrote down your goal. For example, let's say you wrote, "My goal is to write a book about my adventures in Africa."

2. Say that goal either aloud or to yourself several times.

3. Now take the paper on which you've written your primary motivation for reaching your goal, in the case of our illustration it would be, "I want to do something that expresses my creativity."

4. Say your motivation either aloud or to yourself several times.

5. Next, take the picture you drew of what your life will look like when you reach your goal

and stand it on a table or desk at one end of a long room. In the case of writing a book, you might have a picture of you holding a book and handing it to a friend, who's also smiling. [Some people find that simply imagining the way that like will look when they reach their goal is good enough.]

6. S-l-o-w-l-y walk toward the picture and with each step say to yourself either silently or aloud, "I wish I could. . ." and then in your own words describe your heart's desire in the form of a *wish* for your goal. For example, you might say, "I *wish* to write a book about my adventures in Africa."

7. Stand for a moment in front of the picture and notice how your body felt when you said, "I *wish* I could. . . "

8. Now go back to where you started and s-l-o-w-l-y walk toward the picture once more. This time, with each step say to yourself, "I *should* . . . " and then describe your goal. "I *should* write a book about my adventures in Africa."

9. Stand for a moment in front of the picture and notice how your body felt when you said, "I should . . . "

10. Come back to where you started and walk toward the picture a third time. Now as you slowly walk toward the picture of what your life will be like in the future, say with each step, "I *want* to . ." and then state that which you *want* to achieve.

11. Again, notice how your body feels when you say, "I want to . . ."

12. Return to the other side of the room once again and s-l-o-w-l-y walk toward your goal, this time saying,

"I will do whatever it takes to . . ." and then state what it is you want.

13. Stand in front of the picture of the future as you imagine it will be. Feel how your body has experienced the last statement.

14. Now remain standing or sit down and let your feelings settle into your whole body.

When you said *"I will do whatever it takes to . . .,"* did you notice a change in the way your body felt from what you experienced when you first began to walk toward your goal and said, "I wish?" If you did, the chances are good that you are ready to really work toward your goal.

Many people I've worked with find this extremely informative for a very important reason. They realize that wishing is passive. Even though you may fervently hope that things will be different in the future, *wishing* and *hoping* have no more power to affect change than wishes made when blowing out birthday candles.

Thinking you "should" do something is also a poor motivation for achieving success. When others push us to change because they say we *should* or when we feel we *ought* to do something, it's hard to muster the courage and strength it will take to work toward a goal. As I said earlier, pushing is a poor method for change, whether you're the "pusher" or the "pushee."

In the long run, you can only be successful if your motivation arises from deep inside your true self. This is especially true for goals requiring a lot of time, effort, and money. Yet even here, while this attitude at least places your desire closer to your heart, *wanting* must also be connected to your *"will"* in order for you to take action that can make your goal a reality.

TAKE ACTION

Bring a Metaphor to Life

Since going from the Land of Wish-and-Want to the Land of Will-Do is a metaphor, it may take a bit of planning to experience getting through the gate to change so that you experience the greatest benefit from doing the exercise. Here is a suggestion for how you can make the process more of a reality.

Set up a place where you can create a "gate" where you can do this exercise physically. It can be in your house or yard, perhaps the gate can be a door, the area between two chairs, or the edge of the rug and wooden floor. Wherever you want to have a "gate," at that place, or just beyond it, put the picture you made of the future as you imagine it will be when you change your life. Then go through the steps described on the previous page, physically walking through the space you've set up for the exercise.

Once your goal statement fits you perfectly, step across the "line," go through the gate, and begin to work toward your goal and toward changing your life in the Land of Will-Do.

In fact, it has been my experience that it's not until someone can say with great conviction that he will do whatever it takes to reach his goal that he is likely to be successful, or at least successful with the least expenditure of energy.

Where does this "will" come from? As I mentioned earlier, it comes from the central core of who we are, our true selves. When we engage the "will" from that place deep within, we are not *demanding* that we do what we say we want to do. Rather, we are drawing on the power of resolve that resides quietly and firmly in each of us, waiting to be drawn forth so that we might strive toward a worthwhile goal.

Let me tell you about a woman who wanted to stop smoking and discovered that wishing, feeling she should, and even wanting to stop smoking weren't strong enough motivations to stop. As she went through the last step of the exercise, I thought she would finally experience the willingness she needed to begin a plan to end smoking. However, when she said, "I will do whatever it takes to stop smoking," and walked toward the image of a future without cigarettes, she slowly shook her head from side to side. Her words said "yes" but her body and mind said "no." It was then clear to her that she hadn't yet engaged her "will." Without including the true self in the decision to change, she wasn't really going to do whatever it took to reach her goal—and giving up smoking requires a major commitment.

When You're Not Totally Committed to Your Goal

What happens if you walk toward your picture of the future and discover that you don't feel significantly better in saying "I will" than when you said "I wish?" That doesn't mean that you won't succeed. It simply means that it's less likely you'll put as much energy in working toward your goal as you would if you know in every fiber of your body that this is the thing you want to do with all your heart.

Peter's experience offers an excellent example of how important it is to listen to what your body is telling you.

> As you may remember, Peter was sure that he wanted to go to Peru. He felt that the trip was the answer to the problem of not spending enough time with the family.
>
> Then, when asked what he would give up in order to change his life, he said he felt he had already given up a great deal in working less. But when

pressed a little more, he agreed that if he were to remain married that he would have to take off the blinders that kept him from seeing his family's needs. As long as he didn't see their needs, he didn't have to meet their needs.

So he started this exercise by taking a good look at the collage he created and by focusing on the impressive Peruvian mountains.

He and his family were fairly good at hiking and they enjoyed backpacking, but they'd not done serious climbing. Therefore, part way through the exercise he realized there was a good chance they might not be able to pull off that part of his goal and decided mountain climbing was something he "hoped" he could get the family to do, but it may not be possible. [WHEN YOUR GOAL DEPENDS ON THE ACTIONS OF OTHERS, THE POTENTIAL FOR SUCCESS DROPS A FEW NOTCHES.]

So he changed his goal slightly. Next he went through the whole exercise again by saying, "I wish I could . . . should . . . want to . . . will . . . reach my goal of traveling to Peru for a month next year, trekking in the Andes, visiting Machu Picchu and learning how the indigenous highlanders maintain their traditional way of life."

By changing "climbing" to "trekking" Peter made his goal more realistic. Hiking was possible, which his body recognized in the way it responded to the statement that he would do whatever it takes to reach his goal. By the time he finished the exercise the second time, he felt good about his goal. There was a sense of "rightness" about it he didn't have before.

Relief in Discovering the Right Goal

In the TV show "Who Wants to be a Millionaire," contestants have to say, "That's my final answer." Although they may have looked puzzled and uncertain up to that point, when they make their final choice they often sigh with relief and there is less strain visible on their faces. The options are behind them and they have made a commitment. Right or wrong. They can now face the consequences of knowing they have done their best in choosing whatever answer they chose.

If we can go back to Patricia one more time, I'll tell you how this exercise helped with the problem of whether she wanted to change jobs. She didn't have a picture but, instead, imagined she was smiling on a cruise ship, a scene that represented the travel she could do with more money.

At first, she felt positive about moving toward her goal. However, when she said, "I will do whatever I need to do to reach my goal of changing jobs so I can have more money for travel," she stopped and laughed. Then she said, "No. I won't. Money doesn't make me that happy. It would be nice to have more, but to commit to 'doing whatever it takes' is more than I am willing to obligate myself to do." This also changed the rating she gave to having more money in Job B. It went down to a "5" because having it wasn't worth more to her now.

So she stayed in her old job and is "very, very happy" with her decision. Also, her coworkers are pleased she didn't leave. They even brought her candy, a book, and lunch to let her know they were glad she made the decision she made. Since she had already given a "10" for her positive relationship with the workers in the current job, this was frosting on the cake.

If you want your life to change, reflect on this question from CHAPTER SIX:

- *How committed am I to changing my life?*

CHAPTER SEVEN

What Can Support My Efforts to Work Toward My Goal?

Once you're in "The Land of Will-Do," even though you are now ready to enthusiastically navigate the zigs and zags of the goal-reaching process, you're not home yet. As I said in the introduction: "If change were as simple as many claim it is, we could all accomplish our dreams with ease and live in a world of peace. We'd all be millionaires and have perfect relationships."

That is why you should expect the unexpected when you pass through the gate and set out on the path to your goal. Learn to roll with the punches and follow your soul's passion by doing the best you can each day in responding to the challenges along the winding path to success. And to do your best, it helps to discover who and what can support your efforts.

Our hero Roger resembles millions of successful people who have reached their goals in The Land of Will-Do. When they, too, set out to seek their passion or to solve a problem, they were certainly aware of *some of* the obstacles they would face on the far side of the gate. However, they didn't feel they had to have every step clearly understood before they could begin and were prepared to develop the skills they would need to reach their goals. Notice what Roger does in the next stage of his journey.

The Heroic Journey

STAGE THREE

After Roger got past the guardian of the gate by vowing to do his best to learn how to use herbs for healing, we find him standing at the threshold of a great adventure, for his trials and tribulations are only beginning. If you had asked him before he began his journey what he expected to find on the other side of the gate, he would have admitted that he had heard many tales of robbers and vicious animals waiting for those foolish enough to venture into their territory. He's not sure whether those stories were told to dissuade the faint of heart, or whether there was much truth in them.

All he knows is that he had often sensed within himself untested skills and untapped strengths that he hadn't needed back in his home, where life was stable and a future in his father's business was assured. Now he has the chance to test whether he has the qualities of character that will allow him to reach a goal that lies far beyond the comfort of his former life. So he is both apprehensive and a little excited at the possibility of using all his inner resources—and of developing more as they are needed

He begins by asking himself a number of questions in order to find the support all goal seekers need.

If you want to ask yourself the same questions Roger considered after he passed through the gate, you may want to write these down on a piece of paper and use them as a reminder that there are many resources that can help you in the days and weeks ahead.

TO BE CONTINUED

What Small Step Will I Take Today to Move Me Closer to My Goal?

Successful people realize that the problem with trying to look too far in advance is like walking in the woods at night and shining the beam of a flashlight far ahead in order to see where you're going. You're likely to trip if not enough light falls on the ground immediately in front of you. Turn the flashlight toward the ground, however, and you can see what you need to see to take the next step, and then the one after that. If you've chosen the right path, you needn't worry whether you're moving in the right direction. You are. You just have to keep walking.

On the other hand, *unsuccessful* people believe they can't dedicate themselves wholeheartedly to a goal until they know precisely what awaits them on their journey. Before they are willing to proceed, these people want to have all their ducks in a row. Consequently, they never get past the gate. If they do convince themselves that they will do whatever it takes and start out with great enthusiasm, the illusion that they have covered all their bases gets blown out of the water the first time they come across an obstacle they hadn't expected. Consider the slogan of the National Guard: "One weekend a month, two weeks a year." After 9/11, more than one member of the Guard sent to Iraq has discovered how hard it is to predict the future consequences of a choice.

If we try to cover every possible contingency, we can get worn out simply thinking about all the things we *might* need to do on the journey to reach our heart's desire. As a consequence, we often put off the very things we *must* do.

Putting Kaizen Steps Into Action

This is where the Kaizen steps that I mentioned in CHAPTER ONE enter the change process in a very practical way.

Once you have committed yourself to your goal of being your own boss, the first step may be as simple as sending off to the government for regulations on what you have to do to incorporate a business. For the goal of saving money for a trip to Europe, you may want to make your lunch tomorrow instead of eating out, and then putting whatever money you saved into a jar on your dresser labeled "Europe." If you're determined not to argue with your sister, you may decide that the next time you see her you will ask her about something in which you know she's interested, rather than find fault with her lifestyle, which has been your usual pattern. In Peter's

---

TAKE ACTION
Use Kaizen Steps

Each day write your Kaizen step on a piece of paper like a Post-it® note and put it where you are sure to see it; on the bathroom mirror, the refrigerator, the dashboard of your car, your schedule book, your daily to-do-list, your computer. Even better, have several reminders.

To take the idea of Kaizen steps one step further, you can again use the picture you included in the exercise that got you to the other side of the gate. Sketch all or a part of it on each daily note, and don't worry about how it looks. You aren't entering these notes in an art show. All you want is to reinforce your intention to reach your goal.

case, it may mean going to the book store and buying a book on Peru.

Sometimes it may feel that the thing you should do first, such as buy a book, is too easy. You are anxious to get going. That's okay. You're not prevented from taking more than one Kaizen step per day.

But it's easy to become overwhelmed when it feels as though there are three things that are all at the top of your "to-do" list. They are what a friend calls "triorities." You can do three things one after the other, or you could do a little of one, a little of another, and some of the third before starting on the first one again. So it is still important to imagine the jobs on your "to-do" list as Kaizen steps. And remember, you are more likely to stay on the path toward your destination if you don't try to see too far ahead, or have too many "essential" jobs to do at once.

. . . . .

Who Can Teach Me and Help Me Reach My Goal?

Just because you say you are willing to do everything you need to do to reach your goal doesn't mean you have to do it alone! By reaching out to others, you can arrive at your goal's destination sooner, and with far less stress.

Some people can teach you a skill. Others can encourage you to keep going just by giving you a friendly call. Then there are those who have contacts and resources you can tap into, such as the name of a printing company or an inside tip on the hiring practices of a company to which you want to apply.

We all need a cheering section. One way to discover who is in your cheering section is to make a list of everyone in your life who might possibly be interested in what you do. It can include those on the periphery, like the cheerful grocery clerk who always greets you with genuine warmth and a question about how you are doing, as well as the regular folks closer to home. Look over the list and put three stars by those you are sure will be your very best supporters even if you don't ask for their support, two stars by those you are fairly sure will support you if they know you want their help, and one star by those who may not know how to support you, but would wish you well.

Sometimes, however, having friends and family give you a nudge isn't good enough. Even your closest friend is probably not interested in *all* the minute details of what, where, when and how you plan to change your life. It's easy to understand that after awhile your friends will get tired of hearing you say what you *plan* to do, but haven't quite gotten around to actually doing.

This is when it can be helpful to go beyond your usual cheering section and find support you may not have thought of before. As I said in CHAPTER FIVE, it is often a good idea to hire a professional to move you forward. Or a non-professional mentor can help fine-tune your progress. You may find such a person at work or in your church or social group. Perhaps he or she would be honored to give you the pointers you need (but just be sure that individual knows what he or she is talking about). And if you have a talent that the person would appreciate, there may be a way you can exchange services. For example, you could refinish his desk for advice on how to start your own refinishing business. Plus, there are groups for almost every business, hobby and sport you can imagine. Join one and see how much you learn.

TAKE ACTION

Create a Box for Your "Cheering Section"

Find a jar or basket where you can put the names of all those people to whom you've given stars—this is the roster of your support team. On the outside you can put slogans like "Go for it!" "I know you can do it!" "I'm here for you!" "Let's celebrate when you reach your goal."

Then write the names on pieces of paper and put them inside the container of support.

Some days you may want to call one of those people and share your progress with him or her, other times it's just important to know the person is part of your life. A fun way to do this is by going to the box, opening it, closing your eyes, and pulling out one name. Let that name and the image of that person go with you in your heart for the whole day. Remember him or her when you eat, when you go to work, when you sit down at your computer, when you push the lawn mower, when you vacuum the floor, when you stop at a red light. Let the friendship and positive energy coming from that person flow into you.

When Professional Support is Almost Always Needed

There are some goals that are extremely difficult to achieve without support, such as recovering from substance abuse or other addictions.

When you finally make the decision to abstain from alcohol that has caused severe problems in your marriage, and may even have cost you your job, you know in your heart that it takes a day-to-day commitment to keep from falling off the wagon. It's like going to the gate every day and repeating, "Yes, I will do whatever it takes to stay clean and sober today." And as recovering alcoholics will tell you, you may have to make that pledge often during the day.

You have to walk the walk yourself. But you don't have to walk it alone. There are hundreds of thousands of recovering alcoholics who are willing to sponsor you in your recovery efforts. They'll go to the gate with you and help you through. Find a sponsor, find a friend who doesn't support your drinking, and find activities that provide companionship without needing a drink for social lubrication.

People Who Have Already Helped You Are Legion

At breakfast each day, I take a moment before eating and reading the paper to thank those who brought me the food and the paper, as well as other blessings in my life. I begin with a simple, "I give thanks for life." Then I add several more thanks. On one day I may say, "I give thanks for the people who put the paper together for me so I can read what is happening in the world." On another day it might be, "I give thanks for the people who drove the trucks that brought the paper to the distributor who brought it to my door." The next day it might be, "I give thanks for the people who made the cameras that photographers use to take pictures that illustrate the stories I read."

Each day I do something like this for all the people, and sometimes animals, whose efforts allow me to enjoy the food that will sustain me for a morning of work. Each day I change the categories of people I thank. When I do this, I am aware of the widening circle of support that allows me to write and work at my computer. And don't even get me started on computers. When I think of all the people whose efforts have gone into my being able to sit here and type these words, or to surf the Internet, I couldn't count them all — but to all of them I'm grateful.

Therefore, if you ever feel you're alone in working toward your goal, take a moment to think about all the people you don't know who support you behind the scenes. There is the woman you've never met who is working on a new product that you need to reach your goal (if not this goal, then maybe the next one). There is the man who drives long distances to bring to the store the supplies you need for your goal. There is the author who has written a book that explains exactly what you need to do to learn a new skill. You will never meet these people, but you can't do what you want to do without them. The list is endless. Gratitude should also be endless.

. . . . .

What Qualities of the Human Spirit Do I Need to Reach My Goal?

The second question in this book, as you may remember, is, "Am I willing to be totally honest with myself?" Let me tell you about a client who learned the importance of this lesson.

He sat in my office week after week describing a life that was clearly not working. First there was a brief affair with his wife's sister. Then there was the on-again off-again reconciliation with his wife, generally off because he wouldn't follow through on agreements. Next would come the fear that he would have to file for bankruptcy because of overspending, often on items he didn't need. His weight and blood pressure were too high. And the litany continued.

The family history was horrendous, with a father on welfare who sexually abused five out of the seven children (both girls and boys, though my client wasn't one of them) and a mother who admitted to setting one of their rented houses on fire. That was only one of *four* times a house in which they lived burned to the ground!

Trained as a systems therapist, I knew his background played a significant role in who he was and why his life didn't work. Consequently, I used genograms (intergenerational diagrams) and an explanation of dysfunctional family patterns to help explain the origins of his current problems. I also pulled out all the tricks of the trade to help him re-visit, re-experience, and re-frame his childhood so he could "heal the inner child of his past."

Then one day, as we were talking about his latest attempt to circumvent his landlord's attempt to collect rent money, so he could purchase some new stereo equipment, with a grin he casually acknowledged that, "Fabricating my way through life is my modus operandi."

Putting Qualities Into Practice

That's how he and I came to discuss what it means to have integrity, to adhere to an ethical code, to face each day with honor and truth in all he did. Remembering the discussion of his family's dynamics, it was easy for him to see that he didn't have a chance to learn about integrity in the circumstances under which he grew up. After all, he had a father who didn't maintain boundaries with his children—a perfect example of not having integrity as a parent. His mother burned down at least one of their houses—demonstrating a total lack of integrity in maintaining the agreement she had to keep the rental property in reasonable shape!

He became intrigued with this quality, since he'd always been puzzled by how others seemed to get along just fine with telling the truth. "It's like this," I said, "Telling the truth makes life a lot simpler. And since your life is so complicated that it doesn't work the way you want, you might consider

---

QUALITIES OF THE HUMAN SPIRIT

Acceptance, Assertiveness, Balance, Beauty
Carefulness, Clarity, Compassion, Confidence
Courage, Creativity, Curiosity, Energy, Enthusiasm
Faith, Flexibility, Forgiveness, Fortitude, Freedom
Generosity, Gentleness, Grace, Gratitude
Harmony, Hope, Humility, Integrity, Joy, Kindness
Love, Nurturance, Objectivity, Openness, Optimism
Passion, Patience, Peace, Persistence, Playfulness
Purpose, Resilience, Serenity, Simplicity
Spirituality, Stability, Steadfastness, Strength
Tenderness, Tolerance, Vitality

---

giving integrity a try. You've already taken the first step by acknowledging that you aren't truthful. The next step is discovering if you are willing to practice honesty at every opportunity."

He reacted with an interesting mixture of emotions. While there was relief that perhaps he didn't have to continue replaying his earlier life, there was also hope that if this approach worked, he might actually resolve many of the problems he experienced week after week. Overlaid on these reactions was the question of how to practice something he knew little about.

We began with the statement I mentioned in CHAPTER FIVE because I knew it could reinforce his intention to change. At the same time, it acknowledged that he didn't yet know how to use the quality that had been missing in his life. Therefore, I suggested he say, "While I haven't known how to have integrity until now, from this point onward I will practice integrity at every opportunity."

123

And practice he did. The very next week he came in to report that he got a call from a collection agency about unpaid back bills for his pickup truck. Rather than lie and say he sent it two weeks earlier and that they must have lost the check (a statement they might have actually believed because he was quite good at fabricating the truth, having practiced the skill for such a long time), he admitted that he hadn't paid the bills and would be sending a payment that day. Then he actually put the check in the mail!

The consequence of taking this new approach, he said, was that he didn't need to remember to whom he told what, which can get pretty sticky when one always lies.

Therapy didn't continue for long after that because his life began to turn around. There were times, of course, when out of habit he would be halfway through a lie and he'd have to find a way out of the maze he was creating. But all in all, he did a very good job in a reasonably short period of time because he was committed to adding this important quality to his life.

When he came in periodically for a "check-up" session, we sometimes talked about other qualities he might need, but for him the one that was most needed was integrity.

Discovering a Quality You Can Use to Reach Your Goal

Ever since then, I've stressed the need for clients to develop qualities of the human spirit that are missing in their lives. This doesn't mean we shouldn't acknowledge the impact that early experience can have in shaping who we are. It doesn't mean there aren't other factors that need to be addressed. It is simply that a focus on acquiring and expressing qualities can often be as effective as many other techniques in facilitating change.

From goals requiring self-esteem to goals requiring you to

approach a problem at work in a new way, reaching a goal is bound to be easier if you incorporate a quality of the human spirit in whatever you do.

Therefore, in reaching toward your goal, look over the list of qualities of the human spirit at the beginning of this section and notice the quality you will most need. Pay attention to whether you express that quality as often as you'd like.

Sometimes it is hard to select just one quality on which you want to focus. That is certainly the case when I've done this exercise with workshop participants. Invariably several people will insist they can't choose only a single quality because they "need all of them." I assure them that they can

EXAMINE QUALITIES CLOSELY

You can make the most use of qualities if you explore how various qualities have already positively impacted your life. Using "optimism" as an example, notice whether this is a quality you already possess or one that you'd do well to practice.

- *What does optimism mean to me?*
- *Optimism has carried me through difficult situations by _____*
- *I most need optimism when*

  _____

- *The way I express optimism in my life is by*

  _____

- *For me, a symbol that represents optimism is _____*

Now go through the qualities listed earlier and use this as a template to examine any of those qualities does, or could, play a stronger role in your life.

revisit the list later. After all, these qualities don't ever go out of fashion.

Besides, it's hard to focus on more than one quality at a time. Remember the story of Ben Franklin I talked about earlier in CHAPTER FOUR? Follow his example: practice one quality at a time. Of course, if you feel you would do better if you combined two qualities, such as "gentle strength," then go ahead. The only thing you're aiming for is an improvement in some area of your life.

The more often you pay attention to these qualities, the easier it will be to draw upon a quality when you need it. Your already fine character traits will be *expanded* to include another inner resource — one that has always been there, in the core of who you are, but one which you just hadn't noticed before.

· · · · ·

What Image Can Remind Me of My Goal?

Earlier I said that images can be powerful tools for change. Let's take a closer look.

When we see, hear, smell, taste, or feel something, our brains lay down sense images that are used to connect with other similar images stored during previous experiences. These images become the building blocks of our personalities, perspectives and coping styles. Even images buried so deeply that we are not aware of their existence are the lubrication of change and the glue of habit.

In fact, every single thought contains an "image," though we may not think of it as such. Even complex concepts like courage, generosity, love and peace all have images associated with them. And when we laugh at a joke, it is because jokes embody images. We can "see" the banana peel and have an idea of what the man looks like who is walking toward it. When we take part in a political discussion, images influence our convictions.

When considering the impact that images have on your life, it is important not to compare yourself with someone who describes highly colorful images and dreams. Even if you don't believe you "visualize" as well as others when your eyes are closed, the truth is that you cannot *not* hold images in your mind—or surely you would never find your car in a parking lot, remember the face of an old friend, or understand a novel.

> **ASK YOURSELF ABOUT IMAGES**
>
> When I think about success, what image comes to mind?
>
> When I think about failure, what image pops into my mind?
>
> When I think about the effort I need to make to reach my goal, what image comes to mind?

The problem is that much of the time old, unconscious images promote old patterns of thought—leading to old behaviors and giving us old results (supporting that old belief-action-consequences-belief cycle). Even when we realize we must respond differently to a new challenge, even when we've said we will do everything we need to do to reach our goal, the images stored in our minds often are the "default" blueprints we draw upon. If our images are basically positive and self-affirming, our new choices will add to our self-confidence and sense of well-being. If our images are negative and self-defeating, our decisions are likely to lead to further self-defeating behaviors that are harmful to our bodies, minds and spirits.

Fortunately, there is a way to change our images, as more and more people are learning. Clinical research has shown that the ancient techniques of "imagery" and "meditation" can be highly beneficial physically, emotionally, mentally and spiritually. For example, patients are increasingly taught to use imagery as an adjunct to medical treatment to help reduce pain and enhance the body's natural healing mechanisms.

Further, "guided imagery" scripts or exercises can reinforce the life-affirming images of which you already are aware. These techniques can also help you create new images that can lead to new patterns of thought, new behaviors and new results.

If you experiment with several of these techniques, you will most probably find one or two that seem to work best for your needs. Out of any of them may come images that can change your life in the direction you want it to change.

From Images to Action

Several years ago I planned a workshop and knew that someone I admired would attend. I wanted her to like my presentation. But I was afraid I would be nervous and wouldn't do as well as I would have if she weren't there. During that morning's meditation time, therefore, I reflected on the situation and wondered what I could do.

"Easy," replied my intuition. "Just remain calm and everything will go well." Great! An answer I already knew. *Of course* I was likely to do well if I didn't keep thinking about how well I was doing and becoming all tense and bothered by her presence. What I needed was something more concrete, something to keep me from focusing on my performance. That's when I asked myself a question that popped into my head, "How can I remain calm?"

Immediately a flower presented itself in my mind's eye (a lovely gift from my store of images) and I knew that I had an answer I could use. Getting up from my chair, I walked out to the front yard and picked a pretty pink camellia. Then I took it with me to the workshop and placed it on a table in front of the speaker's chair. Whenever I looked at the flower, I smiled inwardly and relaxed. There are times even now when I will bring a photograph of a flower and place it next to my notes. One glance is all I need to restore a sense of calm.

Here is a very simple way for you to access an image that can help you reach your goal:

> *Sit back. Close your eyes. Think about the next step you plan to take in moving toward your goal. Notice if there is something concerning that step about which you have some trepidation. Next, allow an image to arise that can support you when you're actually dealing with the thing about which you are worried.*

You may even want to start each day with a few moments of focusing on your Kaizen step and then allowing an image to appear that can strengthen you as you work on that step. Out of those images may come a symbol, like my flowers, that can reinforce the gift from your best, creative self. With the awareness of the influence of images, let's explore symbols.

. . . . .

What Symbols Can Support My Goal?

In ancient Greece it was a custom to break a slate of burned clay into several pieces and distribute them within the group. When the group reunited, the pieces were fitted together to confirm whether the members belonged to the group. Soon the Greek word for symbol came from two words meaning "together" and "throw," to "throw together," literally a co-incidence. From this beginning evolved our use of "symbolism" to mean an object or sign that stands for something else. These objects can have more than one layer of meaning, and the more profound the symbol, the greater the complexity of the layers of meaning.

Consider the Capitol Building in Washington, DC. It is made of stone, concrete, steel and wood, as are thousands of other buildings. Yet it represents much more than the sum of its individual parts. It embodies the idea and, even more, the "ideal" of our system of government, as flawed as that idea may sometimes be in practice. When we see a picture of the Capitol Building, we respond to the symbolism inherent in how the building is used. Consequently, the Capitol Building of the United States stands for a great, invisible concept—democracy.

Both Common and Simple Symbols Can Have Powerful Effects

While our inner images represent our experiences much like a shadow represents the object that casts the shadow, symbols represent ideas. For example, consider the universally shared symbol of wisdom, the owl—even though owls may not be the smartest bird on the branch!

Advertisements use any of thousands of symbols to remind us of a quality or experience connected with the product being sold, from flags that equate patriotism with the purchase of an American-made car, to happy crews on sailboats that imply freedom of spirit.

Other symbols are part of affirmations and metaphors that catch our attention because they resonate with our experience. One of my favorite comes from a poster that simply had a turtle with the words, "Behold the turtle. He only makes progress when he sticks his neck out."

Often we acquire associations with symbols without being aware that we are acquiring them. When we talk to others, when we read a book, when we write a story, when we sleep and dream, in short, when we engage in almost any activity, our minds continually process the symbols inherent in these activities. They give meaning to communication and to understanding who we are and how we are related to the world around us.

Using Symbols to Support Your Goal

While there is power in universally shared symbols, there is perhaps greater power in those that grow out of personal experience. I can illustrate this with one of my own symbols.

For many years I had flying dreams. If I were outdoors when I left earth's gravity, I would float over the landscape and could look down on beautiful, dark green trees. But there was another kind of flying dream I'm glad I no longer have. In these I would be inside when I started flying and often there would be other people watching, and perhaps pursuing me, as I gracefully flew higher and higher in the building. Almost always I would want to leave, but would be prevented by a locked iron grid or bar over an exit door or skylight.

When I explored the meaning of this dream, I realized that I had given my right to freely make my own choices to others. First it was to my parents and teachers. Then it was to anyone I thought would judge me, which was just about everyone. How could I get past the locked doors and windows? Easy. Own my own key! For several years, I hung a large old iron key over my desk to remind me that I had the power and the right to make my own decisions.

Just as most New Year's resolutions fade with the last notes of *Old Lang Syne*, the pressure of old habits can erode your intention to reach your goal. Fortunately, you have already stated your willingness to do everything you can to reach your goal. Now you have a chance to support your intentions by finding a symbol that can light your way.

The symbol you choose may be one that is often used to

communicate a particular idea. Or you may want to choose an object that would be important to you alone. Whatever your symbol is, it can serve as a powerful reminder of the path you want to follow. How? With a little planning.

For example, imagine you have to attend a meeting that is sure to be tedious and boring. Wear jockey shorts with a crazy pattern (yes, even if you aren't a man). You can have a private chuckle when you think of them, which may even help you find a way to lighten the mood. If you must do something that has always made you nervous, bring a bottle of water you imagine has a relaxing potion. Every time you take a drink, you will become a bit calmer. And if there is someone who tries to bully you, wear a necklace given you by a friend, one who won't let others tell her what to do. Let some of her confidence come through the necklace when you speak to the would-be bully.

> **ASK YOURSELF ABOUT SYMBOLS**
>
> Is there a symbol that has been important to me in the past? Why?
>
> How have I used that symbol?

The possibilities are limitless. Let your imagination run wild.

. . . . .

What Affirmations and Quotations Can Help Me Reach My Goal?

You may have heard somewhere that all you need to do to get whatever you want is to make an affirmation. Declare yourself the person you want to be and you will be that person. Declare you'll have more money and your bank account will increase. Declare you are healthy and your body will automatically be healed.

In my experience, and in the experience of everyone I know, success isn't that simple. That's why I didn't begin this book by suggesting you make such an affirmation, even though I acknowledge that stating an *intention* and having affirmations can give you much-needed encouragement. However, action, as well as intention, has to be part of the success equation. You may want to begin building new neurons and new pathways in your brain by making a statement you would like to be true. But if you

> *In order to profit from your mistakes, you have to get out and make some.*
> – Anonymous

don't do anything to work toward that goal, you will be like a couch-potato who says, twenty times a day, "I am slim," while eating junk food and watching TV.

If you like the idea of using affirmations, and their companion, quotations, be sure to find ones that resonate with you. For example, there is a quotation that is often used to illustrate the need for persistence in striving toward a goal:

> *Nothing in this world can take the place of persistence. Talent will not; nothing is more common than unsuccessful people with talent. Genius will not; unrewarded genius is almost a proverb. Education will not; the world is full of educated derelicts. Persistence and determination alone are omnipotent. The slogan "press on" has solved and always will solve the problems of the human race.*
> – Calvin Coolidge

While there is certainly wisdom in this quote, the problem I have with it is its expression of fierce doggedness. I get weary thinking that, in order to get to a goal I see on the horizon, every day I must press on, plod on, push on, carry on, keep on and persist in moving toward the horizon. That's more pressure to succeed than I want, or need. Consequently, that quotation wouldn't pick up *my* spirits on the road to success. On the other hand, it may perfectly speak to you and give you courage to achieve *your* goal.

> *The best thing about the future is that it comes only one day at a time.*
> – Abraham Lincoln

There are a number of people who use affirmations as a statement of what they hope to have as though they already have it. "I have a perfect job." "I live exactly where I want to live." "My marriage is completely satisfying." They believe this will be accepted by their mind and body as a blueprint of what will happen if they say it frequently enough. I have no argument with anyone who finds this helpful.

> *Success is going from failure to failure without a loss of enthusiasm.*
> – Anonymous

However, while it works fine for some people to say, "I am in perfect health" when they are sick. My brain balks. It thinks, "No, I'm not in perfect health. My body has lots of aches and pains." For me it works much better to say, "I am taking care of my body and it is responding to my care by being the most healthy it can be." This is not only an honest statement of my current condition, it also acknowledges that as I continue to take care of myself, my body will improve.

> *Do what you can, with what you have, where you are.*
> – Theodore Roosevelt

Therefore, my best advice about affirmations and motivational quotations is to only use those that resonate with you. The motivational statement that works for someone else may be entirely wrong for you, just as one image, quality or symbol would work for one person and not another.

Where can you find affirmations and quotations to guide you and keep you headed in the direction you're trying to go? A character in a favorite book may have said something that struck you as something you'd like to remember as you change your life. Many scripture verses can provide just the tone of support you need. And then, of course, the Internet has affirmations and quotations galore. Google "motivation quotation" and you'll find enough for a dozen motivational slogans a day, if you want that many. On the other hand, one may do the trick if it speaks to your particular situation.

> *Let me tell you the secret that has lead to my goal. My strength lies solely in my tenacity.*
>
> – Louis Pasteur

. . . . .

How Can I Slow Down My Frantic Pace When I Have Too Much to Do?

If you set out with enthusiasm in the Land of Will-Do, it can be tempting to include your new goal in your "to-do" list without removing something else. The consequence is that you will not only continue to rush from one appointment to the next and attempt to get as much done in the shortest time possible, as you have probably already been doing, you will now have even more to accomplish. The fact is that you can actually get *more* done in the long run if you learn to move through your activities with grace and ease.

One way to do this, of course, is to take frequent breaks for reflection in your room with a view. After reviewing what is really important and what is not, you can discard many of the things on your "to-do" list that were shoved into your backpack long ago. They are no longer goals you need to accomplish. But there's a good chance you don't take time to do that often enough. Therefore, I suggest a very simple idea that can help remind you of the impossibility of multi-tasking at a break-neck speed.

This idea uses the metaphor of a race with marbles to remind you that you can only do one thing, or possibly two, at a time.

Remember those family reunions where you played games out on a big field and had a grand time cheering on your group? In one of the races you may have been required to carry a Ping-Pong ball on a teaspoon, with one hand behind your back. You weren't allowed to use your thumb to keep the ball on the spoon but had to hurry to reach the finish line, so it was a challenge to go fast enough, yet not too fast.

This exercise uses that general idea, but in this case you'll use marbles. Not real marbles, unless you want to do that, but here the metaphor is to play "the game of life" much as you would if you played any balancing game.

Imagine there are two bowls at either end of a very long room. You begin each day with a certain number of marbles in one bowl and must move as many of them as possible to the other bowl before the end of the day. However, you must move them by using only a teaspoon that can hold, at most, two small marbles or one large one. Your job is to get them from one bowl to the next without dropping them.

This will require you to move carefully if you don't want to drop any, for whenever you drop one, you have to take it back to the first bowl and start again. If you rush too fast, there's a chance you'll lose your marble and it will roll away, causing you to spend time looking for it.

If you move carefully and efficiently, by the end

of the day you may find that you've transferred all the marbles from one bowl to the other without undue stress. There will be no marbles left in the first bowl. You can now relax and perhaps even play a game with the marbles you've calmly moved throughout the day. If you rushed through the transfer job too quickly, however, it's possible you will leave a few marbles in the first bowl and have no time to relax and enjoy your efforts.

Life is like that. Just as there are only twenty-four hours in every day, in this exercise there is a limited number of marbles, each representing the finite time and energy available in any day. When we rush from one appointment to the next, never stopping to smell the roses or allowing extra space for the unexpected, it's as though we are so focused on getting our marbles from here to there that we don't get to play with them. It can feel as though we're Sisyphus, who was condemned by Zeus to roll a stone up a hill for all eternity.

When your "to-do" list is a burden you must get through each day, it it time to remove from your backpack the shoulds and ought-tos stuffed in there years ago. They are only weighing you down with unnecessary work.

· · · · ·

What Incentives Will Encourage Me to Carry On?

This is the shortest section in this chapter because its message can be summed up easily: Life is not a race to see who gets to the end first, or who gets there with the most toys. It is a journey that can be exciting and filled with "delicious ambiguity" as you imagine the pleasure of reaching a goal your true self has chosen. It is also likely not to be exactly the way you have imagined it.

TAKE ACTION

Buy yourself a bag of marbles and a small bowl. Put them on your desk to remind yourself that doing only one job at a time (multi-tasking no more than two activities at once) and moving smoothly from one thing to the next will allow you to accomplish your daily goals and change your life more quickly and efficiently.

However, no matter how long the journey, you can get a bit worn down. That is why incentives can help you walk with a light heart as you take one step after the other and enjoy the view.

One of the first things you can do to keep up enthusiasm for goals that won't be completed quickly is to mark milestones along the way. Right now sit down and write a list of things that bring you pleasure. They can be as simple as sitting in the park and watching children play, going to a movie in the afternoon in the middle of the week, taking your phone off the hook and staying in bed with a good book all day on Saturday, buying a book you've long wanted to own, or taking a bunch of flowers to your mother because she loves fresh flowers in her apartment. The list is endless. Try putting each activity on a separate piece of paper and put the papers in a box or bowl. Then you can take one out every time you come to a convenient point to rest—and sometimes even when it isn't convenient.

Beware, however, that it's easy to set your "milestones" of progress so far apart that you become tired in going from one to the next, even though you know you will be rewarded when you get there. If you only treat yourself when you have accomplished a significant milestone, you may eventually decide that your goal is not worth it. Treat yourself more frequently and you will likely discover that your goal is right for you after all. You just need to pace yourself. And don't forget to give yourself pats on the back more frequently. When your goal is a long way off, remember the words to Mary Poppins' cheerful song, "A spoonful of sugar helps the medicine go down."

. . . . .

What Memories Am I Capturing Today?

When we are focused on achieving success, we can be so single-minded that we fail to see time is passing by without our full participation.

Look around you right now and experience this moment with as many of your senses as possible — seeing, smelling, touching, hearing, tasting, and noticing sensations in your body.

Perhaps there is a greeting card from a dear friend that you have opened on a nearby table, a trophy you received for winning a high school debate, an abstract painting you bought at a seaside resort simply because the bright colors struck your fancy, or any of a hundred things in the room that ordinarily melt into the background. If you have just had a cup of coffee or a cool drink, notice how the flavors linger on the tongue.

Since our lives are filled with many more small incidents than major events, if you consciously experience the pleasures in each moment, you will make an important discovery: by taking the time to "capture moments" you can later retrieve those moments — doubling your pleasure. Then, even on days when many things aren't going well, there are small moments that are, at least by comparison, worth recalling.

If you want your life to change, reflect on these questions from CHAPTER SEVEN:

- *What can support my efforts to work toward my goal?*

- *What small step will I take today to move me closer to my goal?*

- *Who can teach me and help me reach my goal?*

- *What qualities do I need to reach my goal?*

- *What image can remind me of my goal?*

- *What symbol can support my goal?*

- *What affirmations and quotations can help me reach my goal?*

- *How can I slow down my frantic pace when I have too much to do?*

- *What incentives will encourage me to carry on?*

- *What memories am I capturing today?*

CHAPTER EIGHT

What Can I Do When I Get Stuck?

Imagine your goal is to get from one side of a lake to the other. If you think it's shallow enough, you might plan to wade across. If you can swim, you start swimming. Yet what happens if it's very far across, deeper than it looks and/or you don't know how to swim? Then you'd be wise to get a boat or flotation device, or take swimming lessons. If you had none of these, it's clear you'd have a real challenge on your hands if you didn't want to walk around the lake.

Have you ever noticed that some people who set out for their goals are like that? They are so determined to get to where they want to go in the shortest time possible that they plunge right in and start walking, which works fine, of course, until the water comes up to their chins. And they even do well as long as their nose is above water. Then the non-swimmers are in trouble when the water goes over their heads. Even if it's just a few inches, that's enough to stop progress.

There is not a person I know who hasn't at one time or another been bogged down with a project that had originally seemed easy and now is nothing but trouble. We can all misjudge the depth of the water or the distance across. If we didn't think about needing a boat before we started, or if we now realize there are skills we need in order to accomplish our goal, we'll have to take a serious look at whether we should continue, shift direction, or choose another goal that is not as difficult. Once again it is time to ask ourselves some questions, much as our young hero had to ask himself when he was in a similar situation.

The Heroic Journey
STAGE FOUR

Each morning Roger sits quietly and allows an image to form in his mind that can guide him and chooses a symbol that represents his goal for that day. After that, he reads an affirmation that fits the needs for the part of his journey in which he is currently engaged. And along the way he manages to find ways to take time for pleasure.

In remembering his commitment to learn all he can, he's pleased to discover that small Kaizen steps do, indeed, make it easier to build a foundation for success. When he gains one piece of knowledge, he uses that to learn something else. As he goes from town to town, and from healer to healer, he discovers there are many people who want to help him, as well as some who jealously guard their craft and give him misleading information. In the process, despite the long hours of study, he discovers that he's developing strength and courage he had no idea he possessed.

And in many ways Roger has done well. After studying with several people, he has expanded his knowledge of herbs considerably. Before he started, he knew the use of some, but there are many intricacies of healing he needs to master. He still needs to learn how to grow, gather and harvest herbs; how the weather and time of day can influence the potency of an herb; when it is best to take the whole plant at once, including seeds, roots, leaves, buds and blooms, and when he needs to take a part of the plant in a particular order; and when he should use younger, rather than older, plants. There is also much to learn about how to dispense herbs, both internally and externally. For example, which application is best for which ailments? Learning to take full advantage of the healing attributes of each herb is essential if he is to become a master herbologist and healer.

What has him stuck at this point, however, is that he has almost run out of the money his mother gave him the morning he left. Fortunately, he has been offered an apprenticeship that will allow him to study with a well-respected healer for many years. However, in accepting that position, he must continue working there and promise to take over the man's practice when his teacher gets too old to work. This is a real dilemma. While Roger had always assumed he would return to his hometown and bring his new skills with him, he isn't yet ready to go back home because he knows there is much more to learn, otherwise he won't do much better as a healer than the old woman back home.

Roger struggles with his decision. Should he stick with his original goal, which was simply to discover more about herbs, or should he expand his goal and learn as much as he can from this well-regarded healer, but abandon returning to his home? This is when he discovers a series of questions that pull him through to the successful conclusion of his quest.

TO BE CONTINUED

Sometimes Goals Have to Be Postponed

Before examining the questions you can ask yourself when you get stuck, let's look at the last part of Peter's story in the Land of Will-Do, for it is a good illustration of how the path to our goals is not always smooth.

As you will remember, Peter had been confronted by his wife for not spending much time with his family. Thinking a big trip could please his wife, in addition to his willingness to cut his work week from more than 60 hours to "only" 50, he gets lots of information about Peru and what would be needed for the trip—determined to make it an outstanding vacation.

At first, his interest in planning a spectacular trip with the family felt positive to Ellen. The more she thought about it, however, the more she resented his decision to go to Peru without first asking her what she wanted. Even if she did want to go, it was the fact that he hadn't consulted her that made her upset, for it was typical of his barging ahead and making decisions he "assumed" she would accept. The more she thought about it, the more upset she became and finally told him they had to go to marriage counseling. Since she had not withdrawn her threat of separation, Peter decided that might be a good idea and assumed the therapist would see that he was right and get Ellen to agree.

Unfortunately for Peter, that's not what happened. The marriage counselor pointed out that his efforts were consistent with those of a perfectionist who has to work hard and create "perfect" projects so that others would like and admire him. Fortunately, he was able to see that his efforts to do everything well were backfiring and he was willing to spend time in therapy working on his fear of not being good enough. When he got assurance from Ellen that she loved him even if he wasn't perfect, and even if he would make less money by working fewer hours, they decided to postpone the Peru trip. In the meantime, they would break his vacation time into smaller trips that both of them would plan together.

This story illustrates how, in the working-out of a goal, sometimes goals need to be adjusted. It doesn't mean that the original goal was wrong. It just means that there is not always a straight line from planning a goal to carrying it out. As the saying goes, "Life happens while you're busy making other plans." The wise person makes adjustments to the shifts that come his way.

. . . . .

A Dozen Questions for Whenever You're Stuck in Working Toward a Goal

The following questions begin with a re-examination of questions you answered in earlier chapters. By now you have some experience in working toward your goal and your answers may be different than when you first asked them. Because it's important to look at a wide number of issues before you abandon a goal, it isn't until the twelfth question that I suggest you might consider the possibility of choosing another goal. You've put too much energy into the process of change to consider abandoning your goal before asking yourself a few more questions.

In between the first and last questions, there are a variety of questions in no particular order of importance, since the reasons we get stuck vary with circumstances. But all the questions are ones you would do well to ask yourself when you are caught in a bind doing anything. Carefully considering the questions will help you determine whether you are suffering just a minor setback or need to do a major revision of both your goal and your approach to your goal. The answer to a single question is not as important as your answers taken as a whole.

1. *What answers would I give to questions I asked myself earlier, both before going through the gate to change and after I entered the Land of Will-Do?*

   Reviewing your answers to questions in the chapters before you went through the gate to change can remind you of your earlier commitment to change. But if you remain stuck even though your answers to those questions still bring you enthusiastically through the gate to change, you may want to reword the questions concerning support for your goal, which you addressed in CHAPTER SEVEN, such as:

   - What resources and people are available to help me that I haven't yet contacted?
   - Would it help me to identify more things and people for which I'm truly grateful?
   - Are there other qualities I need which I didn't note earlier, but which would be helpful at this point?
   - Are the incentives and rewards I'm giving myself for overcoming obstacles along the path to success sufficient to motivate me to continue?
   - Might other images, symbols, and affirmations support me more effectively than the ones I've been using?

2. *Do I need to lay more groundwork first?*

   Sometimes we stumble because, in our enthusiasm to get started, we've plunged into a task that needed us to first build a better foundation. It isn't that the goal is wrong, but we may need to first put aside more money, build up our strength, arrange for others to take over some household chores, etc.

3. *How did I get to where I am today and what have I learned about reaching my goal?*

    Before you become too hard on yourself, notice what you've been able to accomplish so far. It may very well be that there is something you must first learn, or do, before you can move on. Whatever it is you have to learn or accomplish, I am willing to bet that the lesson will come in handy either in reaching this goal or achieving another goal in the future.

4. *If I merely need to take a break from focusing on my goal, when will I return to it?*

    This is a good question because we can sometimes say we're putting our goal aside "for awhile," when what we mean is that we will put it on the back burner and don't intend to really get around to it until "the time is right." The right time seldom comes if we approach it that way. A better way to look at it is to either reword the goal so that it can be done, or commit ourselves to starting again after a certain period of time.

5. *Have I reached my goal and don't recognize that I have?*

    One of the reasons we sometimes feel we haven't reached our goal, or appreciate it when we do, is that we aren't always sure when we have accomplished it. How do you know whether you've reached your goal? Only you can determine whether or not you've been successful. For example, if you're tired of having your contributions overlooked at work and your goal is to "speak up more in meetings," how often will you have to say something in a meeting in order for you to know you've met your goal? Will it be one comment a meeting, two, three? For a person who's extremely shy, simply saying one thing would be a major accomplishment. For another, it wouldn't be enough. Perhaps it would help to be very clear about what will be noticeable in your life when you've gotten as far as you want to go.

And remember the discussion of first-order change [SEE CHAPTER ONE] and the fact that the progression of moving from one way of being to another takes a lot of small, incremental steps. Perhaps it's time to realize that you have, already, changed greatly. And as you continue with small steps, you will simply move along the same, successful path you've been on all this time.

6. *Am I frustrated because I expected it would be easy to reach my goal? Do I need to have more patience with myself?*

It is not at all unusual for people to expect things will be easier than they are. After all, you've read a dozen books telling you that all you have to do to reach a goal is to work toward it with diligence. But as I hope I've shown, the path to success zigs and zags. You don't know what may be just around the corner and over the next hill. It may be that the part of your journey where you are at the moment is more difficult than it will be later, in which case patience is called for. It may be that you have chosen a goal that is unnecessarily difficult, in which case revisiting your goal is better than giving up. Patience is one of the great qualities of the human spirit and now may be the time for you to make that quality part of the skills you'll use in changing your life.

However, if you are truly struggling and seem to be

getting absolutely nowhere despite all the patience in
the world, then it doesn't make sense to keep going
on to the point of exhaustion. Again, only you know
whether you need greater patience.

7. *What do I think will happen if I go a little further before
giving up?*

There are those who keep going even when they
should stop, when it is clear to everyone else except
them that they have become fanatics who, having lost
sight of their goals, redouble their efforts. They need
to learn how to step back and regroup.

Then there are those who give up too easily at the first
sign of trouble, even though initially they were sure
they would do whatever it took to reach their goal.
Because they can't see around the bend and don't
know what might be coming, they panic and decide
their goals were wrong. The chances are that their
next goals may meet the same fate.

The best way to prevent this is to keep in mind that
often things do not turn out as anyone expects. Not
infrequently, you will find that by going just a bit
further you will discover that what you *hadn't* thought
would happen is exactly what *needs* to happen. This
attitude along the journey of success allows you to see
things from a new perspective and may actually bring
you closer to your goal than you would have gotten if
you had insisted on having the outcome you wanted
at the time you thought it should happen.

8. *Do I need to remind myself of my strengths and the gifts I
will bring to the world in achieving my goal?*

You have something important to offer the world that

no one else can, and the world needs all the gifts it can get. Consider carefully what your gift may be. Hold in your mind an image of how the world will be a little bit better because you have moved a little closer to your goal. And as you continue to change your life, and move toward your goal, you are sure to discover that you have more strengths and qualities of character than you may realize.

9. *Have I allowed unrealistic demands of others, and their opinions, to take precedence over my own goals?*

This can be the case for people who often put the needs of others over their own. If you are a mother or father with young children, you may have to accept the fact that their needs, expressed sometimes as demands, are going to have to be addressed by you. In that case, you may need to get your spouse or partner to help out so that you can work more often on your goal.

However, you will notice that the question says "unrealistic demands." If your goal is really important to you and if you are committed to doing all you can to reach that goal, then now may be the time to take a good hard look at whether the things others are asking of you are realistic and are your responsibility, or whether someone is asking more of you than they have a right to ask.

We are social beings and when we move forward, others may be uncomfortable that we're "leaving them behind." We aren't. We're just changing our lives as our true selves want us to change. Like a mobile in which a movement by one piece affects all the others, change in our lives can make others uncomfortable.

But when we stand by the commitment we've made to ourselves, it is surprising how often others will adjust and, perhaps, find the courage to change themselves as well. So be careful that you don't allow the opinions of others to hinder your progress.

10. *Does my fear that I won't do the job perfectly cause me to procrastinate and not accomplish anything?*

This is a problem of many perfectionists. Perfectionism (the feeling you have to do everything perfect or it's not worth doing) can lead to procrastination (because you can't figure out how to start a project so that it will be done perfectly, or better), which can lead to paralysis (the goal never gets past the gate). It's hard to get past the feeling that you must be "perfect" when striving for the very best has many rewards in our society. It isn't that you shouldn't strive to do as well as you can, but as I point out in CHAPTER FIVE, perfectionists define "doing as well as they can" based on extremely high standards that often are not necessary for the accomplishment of a goal. [SEE "AM I A PERFECTIONIST?" IN THE APPENDIX.]

11. *Is there something else going on in my life that needs my attention or may I simply need to take a break before coming back refreshed and recommitted?*

If you're not making progress, it may be that there is another area of your life you have been neglecting. For example, I am a project kind of person and can get all wrapped up in whatever I'm focusing on at the moment. When I do that, I can forget to pay a bill, call a friend, send a birthday gift to a grandchild, and work later than is good for my body. When the pressure of these responsibilities and needs piles up,

I often notice that I'm not making as much progress as I had earlier. After I take a break, however, I have much more energy, and more ideas, when I return to the project.

If you don't give enough attention to your physical body, your emotional and mental body will suffer. Exercise. Regular meals. Sleep. Relaxation. They are all essential in helping you reach your goal.

Always remember that if you are the one who has set the target date for when you will finish your goal, you are the one who can readjust the time your goal needs to be done. On the other hand, if you are trying to accomplish something that must be finished in a certain time frame, it only makes sense to add some pleasure into your life so your goal doesn't become a burden while you continue working steadily toward your goal.

12. *Is this goal still worth my efforts and is it still consistent with my core beliefs, so that reaching it will add meaning and purpose to my life? If it is not and I need to redefine my goal, how would I state that new goal?*

The very first sentence in CHAPTER ONE makes note of the fact that our lives continually change, so it is not surprising that what seemed important earlier may no longer be important enough to continue along the path on which we've set ourselves. When outside events change, as they are bound to do sometimes, we may need to reevaluate our motivation, the advantages and disadvantages of working toward a goal, etc.

It is not unusual to discover that a goal may have been

the right thing to work toward at one time, but as we make incremental, first-order Kaizen steps, we can change the conditions under which the goal needs to be achieved. Then we may find that we are ready to set our sights on a new goal before our original goal, as we first imagined it, can be completed.

Therefore, to always be sure you're heading in the right direction, frequently take time to step back from the busy-ness of working toward your goal. Get a different point of view. And be sure to visit the room with a view so you may be more aware of your true self and see your goal from a new perspective. Listen to what your heart and soul are telling you. Ask yourself whether reaching your old goal will still give your life greater meaning.

By re-examining the advantages of continuing toward your current goal and the disadvantages of stopping, you may find a new goal that excites you even more than the last one did. For example, Peter did this by creating a new goal, working on himself and his marriage, rather than simply focusing on going to Peru.

You have undoubtedly heard the aphorism that, "If you believe it, you can do it!" As I said earlier, there is a problem in the practice, real world when affirmations give the impression that all you have to do to reach a goal is to only *believe* you can do it.

For example, consider these goals: become President of the United States, win an Oscar, win a marathon, win the America's Cup. Only one person, or team in the case of sailing, can win those races, no matter how much someone *believes* he or she will be the one who wins. Then there are goals that require great good fortune: hoping you'll get into a college with many more applicants than spots available, hoping your new restaurant will be successful in a town with many restaurants, hoping your next child may be the sex you want.

When you look at goals from this perspective, perhaps you may want to revise the idea that believing makes something happen. Certainly if you believe a goal is possible and work toward that goal, you have a far greater chance of success than you will if you doubt you will be successful and go after a goal half-heartedly. That is why I'd like to share with you something I first heard from Carl Simonton, MD, a pioneer in the field of guided imagery for cancer patients. I often mention it with my clients when they wonder whether the effort they are putting into changing their lives is worth it if the ending is uncertain. The statement he made goes something like this: *You can be committed to the process without being attached to the outcome.*

The statement about being committed to the process without being attached to the outcome means that you first need to believe that you could be successful, then work toward that goal, and finally hope good fortune aids your efforts. You are then open to the exciting possibility that either you will get what you want, or you will have an adventure in the process.

· · · · ·

Remember the Lobster

One of the difficulties in moving toward a new way of being is that in the process of change we have to change our identity. Who we "were" is no longer who we "are."

Therefore, whenever we have trouble accepting a changed identity, perhaps we should think about how a lobster sheds its skin. Between molts, a lobster's flesh becomes densely packed within its shell, and a new shell, soft and flexible, is laid down inside the old. To make it easier for the lobster to pull itself out of the old shell, it manages to shrivel the flesh in the appendages to about a quarter of their normal size. Then, just prior to molting, a lobster absorbs lots of water, which causes the new shell to swell, eventually pushing away the old one.

When a lobster sheds its skin, usually it occurs in a burrow where the lobster can be protected until the new shell has hardened. This is important because the soft casing is very vulnerable to attack. Being protected in a cave or burrow during the weeks and months that its shell will take to fully harden allows tissue to replace the water that was gained prior to molting. This gives the lobster the security it needs to fully grow into its shell, so that the cycle of molting and growing can begin again

People are like that. Everyone needs some kind of protection from the world at large. So we carry with us an outward persona, or way of being, that comes to feel quite comfortable over the years. We're used to this old familiar barrier between us and the challenges we face each day. However, throughout life, most of us steadily evolve, shedding old ways and old ideas that no longer fit, often without our conscious effort. Then one day we may discover that we have another persona, another "skin", that replaces the one we used before and are only aware of it when someone points it out to us.

Sometimes, however, we are forced by circumstances to become a "new person" more quickly than we have time to adjust to wearing our latest persona. It is when we have to quickly transition from knowing *who we were* to figuring out *who we are becoming* that we do well to remember how the lobster protects itself as it grows a tougher skin. We, too, sometimes need to step back from all the demands of the world and take time to develop a new way of being that allows us to go out into the world again with strength and confidence.

If you want your life to change and are stuck somewhere on the other side of the gate to change, reflect on the questions raised in CHAPTER EIGHT, all of which can help you answer the question:

- *What can I do when I get stuck?*

Also consider this question:

- *How can I protect myself as I transition from the "old me" to the "new me"?*

CHAPTER NINE

How Can I Share
What I Have Learned?

In most of the great legends of the ages, the hero and heroine come back from their journeys *almost* to the place they left. Sometimes, of course, they will get stuck permanently in a quest, never reaching that which they set out to find. Sometimes they will become enamored with the gift that has been bestowed on them when they finished their final challenge and will choose not to share it with others. Mostly, however, heroes and heroines willingly share with others the boon or reward they have gained through hard work, trial and error, and the blessings that have been bestowed on them.

On the next page you will learn that Roger ends his journey just as heroes and heroines have ended their journeys — by coming back to the town he left, but very different than when he began. You, too, will do the same after you've reached your goal in the "Land of Will-Do," for you will return to your life enriched with the knowledge and experience you've gained.

157

The Heroic Journey

STAGE FIVE

After several years, our hero Roger returns to the gate he left long ago, and stops to visit the gate keeper, as he had promised, to tell him what he has learned in his long journey. When the gatekeeper asks, "Was it worth it?," Roger answers, "I haven't regretted a minute of my time away. I could never have learned what I need to know to be a healer if I had stayed and studied under the old woman who mistreated my brothers. I already know much more than she could ever teach me."

He confesses, however, that one of the times when he felt most conflicted about his goal was when he had run out of money and had been given the opportunity to apprentice to a very wise man. However, Roger would have had to stay there in order to practice what he learned. It seemed as though it was a choice between returning with inadequate knowledge or staying away permanently.

It was then that he asked himself some important questions about what he should do next. There wasn't any one question that decided what he would do, rather, the answers he gave to the group of questions as a whole made him realize that, if he wanted to be the best herb healer he could be, he needed to expand his goal and learn Greek and Latin in order to understand what Hippocrates and other early healers also had to say about herbs. So he set out on a long walk to a city with a university where he got a job as assistant to a teacher, a position which didn't have the strings attached that would have been required by an apprenticeship. Fortunately, he earned enough to keep body and soul together while he continued to gather the vast amount of knowledge he needed.

Eventually there came a time when he again had to decide whether he would stay in the big city and align himself with a university, or come home and become a healer in a much smaller town. The decision to return felt right to him, for he knew that becoming an excellent healer is a never-ending process. It will take many years to build up the practical experience he needs to guide his intuition when choosing the best medicine for each person he treats. That is why, he tells the gatekeeper, he is certain he can study and practice being a good healer as easily in his home town as he could in a big city.

Finally, with confidence and peace of mind, Roger returns to his family. Startled to see him after such a long time, his parents are nevertheless thrilled that he has returned and pleased to have a son who can offer so much to the community. As time goes by, Roger becomes known far and wide as a wise healer who kindly shares his specialized knowledge with all those who need it.

THE END OF ROGER'S STORY

As I said in CHAPTER ONE, life constantly changes. You are likely to find the comfort zone into which you settle yourself at the conclusion of your journey will eventually be less comfortable. At some point in the future, you will once again find yourself pulled, pushed, and prodded by pain to go through the gate and into new adventures.

The good news is that knowing you've gotten through one big change makes the next one easier.

And the biggest lesson you will learn, I believe, is to pay attention to your true self, to the quiet voice within, to the wisdom and guidance that comes from listening to your heart.

Be curious. Ask yourself questions. And while your answers may not change your life dramatically in the space of a day, a week, or a month — after all, some of your neurons will still be entangled in old restricting beliefs — with each successful goal you will be able to move more quickly and easily through incremental changes to a new, more alive way of being.

Most of all, in each journey of change you will surely have learned something that others would love to know — without having to go through all the difficult learning process you had to do.

Best wishes to each of you in finding answers to life's many questions and in sharing what you learn.

Once your life has changed, consider the main question of CHAPTER NINE:

- *How can I share what I have learned?*

Also consider the following "bonus" questions:

- *What question do I believe is the most important question that humans can and should ask? Why?*

- *What question do many people often seem to ask that I believe is the least important? Why?*

- *What is more revealing about an individual, the questions a person asks or the answers he or she gives? Why?*

APPENDIX

AM I A PERFECTIONIST?

In this simple quiz on perfectionism you will notice that I haven't included a score card to grade yourself. You don't need *someone else* to tell you if you're a perfectionist. If you are one, you *know*. At least you do if you're honest with yourself. And as the CHAPTER TWO points out, the journey to change begins with honesty. Therefore, just as acknowledging you're an alcoholic is the first step in recovery, acknowledging you're a perfectionist is the first step in taking some of the pressure off your life.

A Self-Test on Perfectionism

1. Do I like to prove my value as a person by showing others I am totally competent at some task? Why?

2. Do I attempt to enhance my position at work or with others by pursuing tasks and making certain others know how well I have done? If so, why do I think this is so? If not, why not?

3. Do I tend to believe that others want me to achieve something well and that they have high standards for me even if they don't say it? Why?

4. Am I impatient with my own errors and notice that images of past failures plague me?

5. How do I keep reminding myself of what I haven't done well enough?

6. Can I separate striving for excellence, which is

sometimes possible to attain, and striving for perfection, which is not? If so, how do I manage to remind myself of this difference when I am in the middle of an important project?

7. If someone complains that I am being a perfectionist, what is my response? Why?

8. If someone makes a comment about a topic of which I know something, do I feel I have to make certain they know I, too, know about it? If so, why?

9. Do others complain that the standards I set for them are two high? How accurate might that accusation be?

10. When have I tried to do a job perfectly (though I may tell myself that I'm just aiming to do a "very good" job), then postponed the job because I didn't have all the steps laid out to do it "right," and then became paralyzed at the prospect and ended up not doing it at all? How often does this happen to me?

11. Do I often feel that nothing I do will ever be enough?

12. Do I often behave as though everything I do is going to be inscribed on my tombstone? If yes, do I feel this way more than I'd like to admit?

13. If I don't get a project finished in the time I've given myself, do I assume there is something wrong with me?

14. Do I often complain about the incompetence of others?

15. Do I avoid doing the things I can't do well?

16. If someone doesn't compliment me on a job I thought I did well, does it make me not only disappointed,

but angry, even though I would never express it?

17. Do I feel guilty about many things that other people wouldn't feel guilty about doing?

18. Do I feel proud of what I say and do and think others should realize I am clever, and praise me for it?

19. Do I think others won't like me if I don't do the best job that can be done on a project?

20. Do I let others know that I know the answer to a problem or question, even if it isn't essential they know that I know the answer, so they won't think I'm dumb?

21. Am I uncomfortable in situations where no one is in control and try to take control if I can?

22. Do I expect others will praise me for what I do and am I disappointed when they don't?

23. Do I identify myself as a perfectionist? Why?

ABOUT THE AUTHOR

Arlene Harder received a masters from California Family Study Center and is a licensed marriage and family therapist who enjoyed a private practice for more than twenty years in Pasadena, CA. She is also a member of the California Association of Marriage and Family Therapists and the American Association for Marriage and Family Therapy.

Out of her work with parents of grown children, and her personal experience, she has written *Letting Go of Our Adult Children: When What We Do Is Never Enough*. Together with Jane Toler, PhD, licensed professional counselor in Dallas, Texas, she is creating a national program for healing strained and broken relationships between parents and adult children.

Before entering graduate school, she was certified in Psychosynthesis, a holistic school of psychology. She later studied with the Academy for Guided Imagery and has developed many imagery exercises that use imagination and mental images to help people get in touch with their strengths and inner resources. Using these techniques, she has led many workshops for people dealing with serious illness and co-founded The Wellness Community–Foothills, part of a national psychosocial support program for cancer patients and their families. She also co-founded CancerOnline, a nonprofit website and served pro-bono as executive director for five years.

Now Arlene Harder has created three other websites for which she writes extensively and has produced several flash and animation features, a Q-and-A Club, special features, and online workshops. She hopes that her efforts, together with the efforts of others, will help create a better world.

The author can be contacted through:

www.support4change.com